Finding my Lifesaver

A Swimmer's Journey through Success, Breakdown, and Finding Balance

*Becca!
Good Luck & Have Fun!!
♡,
Kristen Woodring*

KRISTEN WOODRING

To my father and mother . . .
Ron and Geri Woodring.

Copyright © 2008 by Kristen Woodring
All rights reserved. No part of this book may be reproduced, stored, or transmitted by any means—whether auditory, graphic, mechanical, or electronic—without written permission of both publisher and author, except in the case of brief excerpts used in critical articles and reviews.
Unauthorized reproduction of any part of this work is illegal and is punishable by law.

ISBN: 978-0-557-07839-4

Finding My Lifesaver

CONTENTS

ACKNOWLEDGMENTS 3

Introduction 5

Chapter 1: Discovery 11

Chapter 2: The Rise to Stardom 17

Chapter 3: The Summer of Change 27

Chapter 4: National Record! 35

Chapter 5: Swimming My Best 43

Chapter 6: Super Star? 53

Chapter 7: Sinking 63

Chapter 8: Desperate for a Life Saver 73

Chapter 9: Retirement 83

Chapter 10: The Comeback 91

Chapter 11: One More Year 103

Chapter 12: Ending on a High Note 111

Tips for Parents, Coaches, and Teammates 117

ACKNOWLEDGMENTS

Ron Woodring – To my father . . . Thank you for all the guidance and encouragement you have given to me my entire life. I love you.

Geri Woodring – To my mother . . . Thank you for always being there to support me, even when I wasn't the easiest child to deal with. I love you.

Angela Mitstifer – My big sis . . . I appreciate your silent leadership and having such an amazing older sister to look up to. Your advice has never gone unnoticed.

John Pontz – Thank you for opening my eyes to my natural gift and showing me that I was destined to do great things . . . all I needed to do was believe in myself.

Bill Dorenkott – Through good times and bad, I am thankful for having you as a leader and mentor. Thanks for standing by me during a rough time and helping me learn how to balance everything.

Wilson High School Family – Thanks for the support. I will always remember the great moments and fun times.

Penn State Teammates – To all of you that I swam with and those who came before and after my time at PSU . . . Thank you! You have helped me become the woman I am today. Never forget that we are part of something special and so very lucky to bleed blue and white.

Melinda Copp – My ghostwriter and friend. Thank you for helping finish something that I have dreamt about. It was a wonderful experience working with you and I truly appreciate all that you have done.

Introduction

For athletes, there's nothing like the feeling of winning and seeing all your hard work pay off in a big victory. I started swimming competitively when I was six years old. Training and working hard have always been a part of my life, and I swam miles and miles over the years so I could feel the sense of accomplishment and satisfaction that comes with winning. But when I won my second Big Ten title in the 100-yard breaststroke as a sophomore at Penn State, I hurried away from the mob of my teammates, coaches, and family members celebrating my victory to hide in the locker room and cry.

For many people athletics and extracurricular activities are a huge part of childhood and growing up. The memories and friendships made while participating can play a major role in a child's development. Throughout my entire childhood, I was very active. I participated in swimming, gymnastics, basketball, softball, and track. I also played the piano and sang in the choir. Swimming was the one activity that I stuck with and truly found thrilling and exciting. During my swimming journey I learned many great life lessons and developed numerous qualities. I learned what hard work, determination, dedication, perseverance, and passion can do for an individuals' life. Many of my behavioural traits, I believe, are inherited and have been with me since a young age. The whole argument of nature versus nurture is relevant in athletes. For example, I have always been a competitive person and intensely driven. Whether I would be swimming, doing school projects, or playing with my sister, I would always want to be the best. Those characteristics helped me accomplish many great things in swimming and my personal life.

When I reached my teen years, my swimming times started getting faster and while seeing that improvement I also enjoyed the daily grind of the sport. Before the age of eighteen, I swam for my country in two international events, broke a high school national record, was named Female High School Swimmer of the Year, and was offered a full scholarship to numerous Division 1 colleges. Every accomplishment motivated me to continue to train harder and set higher goals. I loved to push myself. I also enjoyed competing and reaping the rewards of all my sacrifices.

By the time I was twenty years old, a lot of the pressure my coaches, parents, teammates, and I put on myself caught up with me. I hit a wall—my swimming times got worse and my emotions became uncontrollable. I stopped feeling the rush of adrenaline and excitement before my swimming races. That was when I started to develop signs of career burnout and I fell into a deep depression. I struggled with failure and authority. I lashed out at my coaches and teammates and started to surround myself with negative people and influences. I also struggled with learning how to deal with new and different emotions towards a sport that I had always loved and been so comfortable participating in. I found myself saying I hated swimming and I could not stand to be around my team, my coaches, and the pool. Those emotions were completely out of the ordinary for to me. Swimming had always given me confidence and self-esteem and for the first time it was doing the complete opposite. It was making me feel worthless and alone. A few months after Big Tens my sophomore year, I gave up my full scholarship and all the glory that went with it and quit swimming. And after all those years of being viewed as a huge success by everyone around me—my parents, my teammates, my peers, and my coaches—I left my team and was viewed as a quitter. But I was so burned out that I couldn't stand the smell of chlorine. And I stayed like that for months before I realized I was more than an athlete, and whether I won or lost a race didn't have to define me as a person and control my happiness.

That was years ago, and I've changed a lot since then. I eventually came back to the sport with a clear head and finished my career by earning my fourth Big Ten title. Although I don't compete anymore, I still swim for exercise. I work for Dolfin Swimwear and I'm still involved in the swimming community. When I travel for work I meet swim families who are a lot like I used to be. I can see their intensity and dedication to the sport, and I see a piece of myself in each of them.

I believe that having an intense drive and dedication to a sport, hobby, or special interest is a blessing. I also believe that if you find your passion in life, you must recognize that failure will occur at some point in time. Being able to accept failure, learn from it, and grow is the key to success. For example, many people join swim teams, soccer teams, drama clubs, or whatever and do not experience an intense emotional high when they win, succeed, or excel. They simply choose to play a sport or join a club for the experience and fun of doing it. They can separate their self-worth from that activity. It is only one part of their life. They do not let the activity define who they are as a person. I, on the other hand, depended on swimming to give me confidence, self-esteem, and meaning. My life had no balance. I didn't understand how to live life and enjoy it without the sport of swimming. And when I put so much pressure on myself to always win and improve, I couldn't handle swimming anymore and I felt like I was left with nothing.

When a child shows athletic promise, which often starts at a young age, many parents start thinking about college scholarships and athletic careers. They want to know what it takes to raise a child that can compete at a high level. And when the parents I meet when I travel for work find out that I once broke a minute in the 100-yard breaststroke, I placed fifth in the Olympic trials, and I won four Big Ten titles, they ask me questions like, "Should my ten-year-old daughter be swimming six days a week?" "How can we find the right coach?" "Should we put her in this swim club, or that one?" I hear these questions all the time, and I tell the parents what they want to know. I tell them about how dedicated and competitive I was and how I switched clubs to find the right coach. Coaches have such a big influence on athletes that athletes have to really trust the person if they want to improve.

But I also remind them to let their kids take a break. It's okay if they don't swim every day for ten years. Taking breaks every once in a while is helpful—both mentally and physically. And if a child doesn't want to go to swim practice one day, then take them for ice cream or a movie instead. Life doesn't have to revolve around swimming, especially at such a young age. When I tell parents about my year off, how I was burned out, and how my break actually taught me a lot about myself and my love for the sport, some are really interested. But others hear the word "quit" and just view it as my own personal weakness. Burnout, depression, and mental health carry a stigma in sports, particularly at the higher levels. Athletes are expected to be strong. No one really talks about mental health in athletics, and many people don't understand what a difficult challenge the mental side of sports can be, even though athletes who seem to be at the top of their careers struggle with these issues all the time.

When I started researching sports and mental health, I was surprised to find out that even though burnout and depression are common among athletes, the topic is taboo. "Prisoners of Depression," an article written by L. Jon Wertheim for Sports Illustrated in 2003, describes several elite athletes who were isolated by their conditions. Jim Shea, a world champion bobsledder, said he felt empty when he won a spot on the 2002 Winter Olympic U.S. Team.

"It was total emptiness, like I didn't even care," he told the reporter. "The joy of winning? I could have broken a world record and won the lottery on the same day and not been happy about it." The article explained that Shea came from a family culture of strength and stoicism, and when he was diagnosed with depression by a U.S. Olympic Committee psychologist, Shea's reaction was: "Me? Depressed? How could that be? I'm an athlete."

Ricky Williams, the NFL's 2002 rushing leader, suffered overwhelming social anxiety from a young age. Through college and into professional football, the article suggests, the problem was exacerbated by his success and the attention it drew. When he injured his ankle playing for the New Orleans Saints, a team of trainers and rehab professionals checked on him almost daily, but no one noticed his antisocial and avoidance behaviors.

"There's a physical prejudice in sports," Williams told Wertheim, "When it's a broken bone, teams will do everything in their power to make sure it's okay. When it's a broken soul, it's like a weakness."

Although I was never medically diagnosed with depression or another mental illness, I experienced several of the symptoms: trouble sleeping, anxiety, feeling out of control, mood swings, low self-esteem, lack of motivation and interest, all-or-nothing thinking, social withdrawal, trouble with authority, and crying episodes. When I look back on everything that happened to me and the way the events unfolded, I know I went through a mental breakdown, which is defined as a sudden, acute attack of mental illness, such as depression or anxiety. The term is not recognized by the psychological community because it has negative connotations, but this phenomenon is a normal and relatively common response to chronic stress. Often, the breakdown is a manifestation of career burnout.

I was most likely born with my strong desire to compete. Swimming and the successes I experienced starting with that first lap in the pool heightened my ability to set, work toward, and achieve goals. These personal characteristics combined with pressure from others to succeed drove me to huge achievements, and also to an unbalanced, unsustainable career. Everything in my past led me to the moment when I was at the peak of my career and all I could do was cry. I was lucky, though, having been able to pull myself out of my burnout and feelings of depression and finish my career on my own terms.

When I look back on my story, it's obvious that all the events in my career, which are described in this book, led me to that breakdown my sophomore year in college. The signs are so clear to me now, but no one ever noticed them then. Perhaps if they did, I could have avoided some of the hardships in my career. And of all the bits of advice I give swim parents, athletes, and coaches today, I most want them to understand how to recognize the signs and avoid burnout in young athletes that could prevent them from fulfilling their potential and enjoying their sport.

Chapter 1: Discovery

When I jumped in the pool for my first swim practice, I never thought swimming would become such an important part of my life. And I didn't realize I'd grow to love swimming more than anything, or that, at times, I'd hate it so much that I never wanted to get in the pool again. On that summer morning in 1988, I was just a chubby six-year-old excited to have something to do.

My parents, who always wanted to give my sister and me as many opportunities as possible, signed us up for the Muhlenberg Swimming Association primarily to develop my sister's athletic talents. Even at eight years old, she had the body of an athlete with broad shoulders, defined biceps, and strong legs. She never worked out at that age; we were just normal kids. But she was very muscular and just looked like an athlete. We had both been taking gymnastics lessons for a few months prior to swimming and my sister excelled at it without much effort at all. I was more of a tagalong, and not very athletic. But that didn't bother me.

The morning of our first practice, there were about thirty or forty other kids all standing around the pool in their suits, goggles, and swim caps. I didn't know very many kids my age at that time, and was excited swimming would give me the opportunity to meet a few. Practice started early in the morning and a slight chill hung in the air. And when the coach yelled for us to hop in and start warming up, everyone splashed into the water. The pool was heated and the water felt better than standing outside in my bathing suit, but when I looked back I saw my sister still standing on the edge, crying. She didn't want to get in.

My sister was always more quiet and reserved than me. She never liked to be the center of attention and preferred reading to athletic competition. So while I was swimming my first laps in the pool, my mom was on the side trying to convince her to get in the water. I can remember wondering, "What is the big deal?" Why couldn't she just get in the water? Looking back, I think she was afraid it would be cold, and she probably felt a little vulnerable and unsure. The temperature outside was about fifty-five degrees before the sun came up, and when it feels that cold and you're wearing nothing but a bathing suit, jumping in the water is the last thing you want to do. But I was fine, and I wanted her to try it. Eventually she did get in. And although she wasn't always as willing to try new things as I was, her innate athletic abilities shined as soon as she started swimming.

We practiced swimming for three or four weeks before meets started. As beginners my sister and I learned freestyle first. Once we got the hang of that, we learned the backstroke. Then we learned more complex strokes like the butterfly and the breaststroke. During swim meets, my sister showed her natural talent and won effortlessly. She never got too excited, but when she would dive in to race, she blew her competition away. She was stronger than all the other kids, but when it came to competing, she could take it or leave it.

I developed a little differently. At the first swim meet, my coaches noticed that I wasn't diving correctly. Instead of sliding into the water in a smooth line, I did more of a belly-flop. So after practice, I started staying a few minutes late with one of the coaches to work on it. We met to go over techniques for diving without hurting myself—and I was determined to get it. I don't remember ever being frustrated with myself, but I know I didn't think about anything else until I got it. All the other kids knew how to dive, and I was excited to be like the other kids. I looked forward to the end of every practice so I could work one-on-one with the coach. When practices ended and all the other families started eating lunch and the kids started playing together, I practiced on my own at the side of the pool. And it took a couple weeks before I finally did it. Learning how to dive was the first time I worked toward a goal and achieved it, and it gave me such a feeling of accomplishment to see my hard work pay off. And once I figured it out, I couldn't stop diving.

At the end of the summer, our team held a banquet and awards ceremony to close the season. All the kids on my team and their families came for the picnic at the pool pavilion—probably a hundred people were all sitting on the picnic benches. We ate lunch and then our coaches lined up at the front of the pavilion to present the awards. They announced winners for the highest number of total points, MVP, most spirited, and several others. For each award, they said a few words about the swimmer before revealing the name and if I wasn't distracted by something else, I tried to guess who they were talking about. Then when the coach announced the name of the swimmer, everyone in the pavilion clapped and cheered. As a beginner, I looked up to all the experienced, older swimmers. And I was excited to see my teammates win their awards.

When they got to the last award for the "Most Improved," the coaches said this swimmer was very determined all season and always kept a positive attitude. Then they announced the name: "Kristen Woodring." I was so surprised to hear my name, and everyone in the crowd cheered as I walked up to shake hands with the coaches and accept my award. I couldn't believe it—all I'd done was figure out how to dive off the block. I was so young, but I felt so proud. Winning that award was the first time I had really won anything. I realized that I enjoyed working on my weaknesses, such as diving and finishing one lap, and seeing the hard work pay off instilled a passion in me for the sport of swimming.

As my first swimming season ended, many parents and coaches informed my family that if my sister and I really want to improve and become serious about swimming, we needed to swim all year round. That meant finding a winter swim team.

Around this time my parents sat both my sister and I down and asked us to choose between swimming and gymnastics, which we had done the previous winter. My sister was really good at both, and my parents said they wanted us to focus on one sport because swimming would keep us busy all year. A few months before, one of our gymnastics coaches said to my mom that my sister would need to slim down if she wanted to get serious. This, when my nine-year-old sister didn't have an ounce of fat on her body, kind of turned us away from gymnastics. It was fun, but I was too little to do anything but rolls on the floor. And so we focused on swimming.

That winter, my sister and I joined the local Reading YMCA. We knew other families in that program and they recommended it to us. We needed to swim all year if we wanted to improve, and winter swimming was much more serious than summer. The pool was indoors and bigger, and about three times as many kids swam on the team. We practiced almost every day, and even the practices were competitive. We were swimming against our teammates, with eight kids in each lane, but we'd all try to be the first one to lead the lane. I started looking forward to practices and also to racing at meets on the weekends. After a few months, instead of just finishing races and getting last in my heats, I started placing fourth and even third, which was a great improvement from summer.

And while my sister had all the physical advantages, I had a fire to compete. One meet I remember in particular was the Invitational Swim Meet at the York YMCA. The meet was on a weekend, and it lasted all day. I was still six years old and entered to swim the 100-yard individual medley (IM) for the eight-and-under age group. The IM was a combination of strokes—butterfly first, backstroke second, breaststroke third, and freestyle for the fourth and final lap. This particular race probably had six heats of eight girls, so I lined up behind the block with the other seven swimmers and waited for my heat. I was in one of the middle lanes and next to me, lined up to swim in my heat, was the biggest eight-year-old girl I'd ever seen.

I've always been average sized, but this girl was tall and muscular, just like my sister, who swam in a higher age group. Seeing who I was up against, I got a little nervous. She was at least four inches taller than me, and seemed like a twelve-year-old. But I set my mind on swimming as fast as I could to beat her and win my heat. I looked over to my mom and dad, gave them a quick wave (a signature move of mine until I was about ten years old), and got up on the starting block. The gun sounded and I dove into the pool. When I popped up and started the butterfly stroke, all I could think about was moving my arms as fast as they would go. And I watched the big girl from the corner of my eye the whole race. In swimming, you can't look directly at the competition because turning your head because it creates drag in the water. But I could see her shoulders and cap ahead of me through my peripheral vision. Each lap became more painful, but I did not give up. I was behind her the whole time, but on the last lap, I swam harder than ever before in my one-season swimming career. I turned my arms over and kicked my legs as fast as I could, until I hit the wall and finished.

I don't even think I checked my time afterwards, and I was so young that I wouldn't have known what time was good or bad even if I had asked. I remember I was so tired and my arms were so weak that I didn't have enough strength to pull myself out of the water. One of the timers on the pool deck reached down and gave me a hand. I immediately walked over to my parents—as I did after every race. I looked up at my dad and said, "My body hurts all over." He just wrapped a towel around me and gave me a hug.

I placed second to the giant—by far my best race. Even though I had been determined to win, I don't remember being upset or disappointed. Swimming at that point, and for many years later, was always a positive, exciting experience for me. And I knew that if I worked hard, I could do better the next time.

Years later, my dad told me that when he saw me swim so hard that day at the York YMCA, he knew there was something special in me. You can't teach passion, drive, or competitiveness. I was a fearless athlete, even at such a young age, and when I raced I put forth a great deal of effort to beat whoever was swimming against me. Even at the age of six, when I'd been swimming for less than a season, I had a strong passion to compete and be successful.

I also enjoyed the lifestyle associated with swimming. Aside from frequent practices, I liked eating healthy pasta and going to bed early before meets. I liked traveling on the weekends and spending the whole day playing cards and hanging out with the other kids while we waited for our races. And I loved the feeling of my adrenaline increase when I stepped on the blocks to swim and compete.

With such frequent practices and meets, swimming eventually took over our dinnertime conversations. My parents got to know other parents sitting in the stands at meets and we started spending time with other swimming families outside of practices and events. It started that first summer and snowballed from there—swimming quickly became a major part of our lives. And by winter, we had become a dedicated swimming family.

Chapter 2: The Rise to Stardom

All swimmers have a best stroke. When I was nine years old, I started making the A relay team to swim the butterfly leg. My coaches saw during sets at practice that butterfly was my strongest stroke, and not many other girls on the team could do it well, so I became a butterflier. That didn't last long, though. At eleven years old, while swimming for a summer club, our team's breaststroker couldn't race in the 50 breaststroke at one of our dual meets. She may have been sick or out of town that day, I don't remember exactly. But they needed someone to fill in for her, and so the coaches put me in the event. I'd always known how to swim all the strokes fairly well, and I'd swum them all in the IM. So I swam the 50 breaststroke, and that one event changed my career. Not only did I win the race, but I set a team record as well. After that day, I was a breaststroker.

As I got better and better at swimming, my parents were a consistent support system for me. They always took my sister and me to practice and swim meets. And most of the time I looked forward to swimming. But if I wanted to do something else rather than practice, my mom and dad would say, "You made this commitment to swim, we're going."

After swimming at the Reading Y for nearly seven years, I changed clubs. In the swimming world, YMCAs only swim other YMCAs. We switched to a United States Swimming (USS) club because we'd have more opportunities to compete at a higher level. This decision didn't come easy for me. All my friends swam at the Reading Y, and although some went to my school, leaving meant I was giving up the team I'd known for my whole swimming career up to that point.

The decision to change clubs was also a turning point in another way. When we started swimming in the first place, it was because my sister had athletic talent. I had been the tagalong. But we changed clubs because I was becoming so good and was so dedicated to the sport. My sister treated swimming differently than I did, and my parents treated her differently as a swimmer—it was no big deal if she missed practice. She chose to have a life outside the sport, while I had the most fun when I was hanging out with my swimming friends. My parents saw how driven I was, and wanted to support me in advancing my swimming career. At the time, I had just turned thirteen and every time I got in the pool, I swam a little faster. But my parents felt like my progress had come to a stand-still at the YMCA. I had recently missed the Junior National cut by one second, and having gotten that close, we knew I could make it. I just needed the right coaching to get me there. Making the Junior National cut is the first step in making the Olympic trials—in other words, I was very close to a very big meet. Up until that point, I had always swum locally and regionally. But a whole world of highly competitive swimming existed beyond Pennsylvania. My first time swimming outside local clubs was when I swam on the Mid-Atlantic Zone team. There, all the kids had their sights set on Junior Nationals, and eventually the Olympics. After seeing all these new opportunities, I started taking swimming more seriously, setting goals, shooting for specific times and meets.

My eyes were opened, and so were my parents'. They learned what else was out there, and realized I was a better swimmer than they previously thought. And they wanted me to take it as far as I could. With so many kids at the Reading Y, my parents and I realized that if I wanted to work to my full potential, I needed to swim at a club where I could get more individual attention from the coaches. Although the Reading coaches were wonderful, the program was big and getting bigger. The coaches had so many kids they couldn't focus their attention on any one swimmer for long.

After leaving Reading, we tried the Central Penn Aquatic Club, CPAC, in Harrisburg. But I didn't swim there for long because it was over an hour from our house and the drive every night to practice was too difficult. Around this time, we heard about a new coach at the Lancaster Aquatic Club. John Pontz, at twenty-six years old, was a new, young coach. He didn't have much experience or an ego. He was a former swimmer himself, but struggled with injuries and never reached the level he would have liked. However, everyone in our swimming community noticed him because when we swam against Lancaster at meets, almost every swimmer on the team had improved under John's direction. One athlete in particular caught my parents' attention—a boy named Kyle, who was also a breaststroker. My parents thought that if the new coach could help Kyle improve, he might be able to help me too. With Lancaster only a half-hour from home, the drive would be easier and I switched clubs. And although I didn't realize it right away, this decision changed my life.

Being the new girl is never easy. I had seen the girls on the Lancaster team at meets and their faces and names were familiar, but on my first day of practice with them I wasn't sure if they would accept me as a part of their team or not. Even though we were all swimmers and athletes tend to have a quiet understanding of other athletes in their sport, thirteen-year-old girls don't always accept each other with open arms. And I got quite a few that's-the-new-girl stares when I entered the locker room my first day on the team. After changing, I walked up the stairs to the pool by myself and found John waiting for me outside the locker room door. Although my parents had talked to him before, I never had. As he walked me down the pool deck to the blocks to start practice, he asked me about my day at school. Sometimes coaches can be a little intimidating, but not John. He seemed genuinely interested in getting to know each kid on the team as a person, not just a record of swimming times. And with such a small club—about a quarter of the number of kids on the Reading team—he could give each athlete special attention. He thrived on seeing his athletes improve, and he had such a passion for the sport of swimming. From that first day of practice, I loved swimming with him. And my swimming started to improve right away, too.

Usually when you change clubs or start working with a new coach, it takes a while to adjust to the different workouts. But John's coaching style clicked with me right away. Swimming at Lancaster was basically the same as the Reading Y—the kids were the same and practices were the same. The only difference was John. He showed a passion for learning and being the best coach he could be. He had no problem calling fellow coaches to ask for advice and help. He also focused on each of his swimmers as individuals. Every Saturday morning, John had the senior team (the high school kids) over to his house for breakfast and he made each swimmer feel like they were someone special and an important part of the team, whether they were the best swimmer on the team or not. And he was the first coach I could ever laugh and joke around with. That's just the way he was. If I was stressed out about school or anything else, John would never let me get in the water unless he talked with me. He made me want to be a better swimmer and, therefore, I trained harder than I ever thought was possible. After training with John at Lancaster for just three months, I made the Junior National cut by a few tenths of a second. I didn't beat the time by much, but I made it during one of the first few meets of the season. This was a great accomplishment for a fourteen-year-old and I planned on it being the first of many goals obtained.

That school year, my eighth grade year, I was the manager for the high school swim team. This was really exciting for me because my sister, who was in eleventh grade, was on the team, and I loved being around all the older swimmers. My high school, Wilson, had a competitive team, and swimming was one of the most popular sports in my area. Being the manager let me be a part of the action before I was old enough to swim on the team. The coaches let me help out during home meets by taking splits, filling water bottles, and working the timing system. I even got to travel with the team for a few meets. My sister was friends with everyone on the team, but I was more the quiet observer just waiting for my chance to swim at their level. I felt like it would be a lifetime before it was my turn to be on the relays and sit on the bus with all the girls on the team.

Aside from getting a glance of high school swimming before I got there, being a manager meant I got to witness Kristy Kowal, in her senior year, break the High School National Record in the 100 breaststroke. Kristy Kowal was an amazing swimmer who years later won a silver medal in the Olympics. But even in high school, everyone knew she would be a star. She broke records practically every time she got in the water. Every swimmer in the county looked up to her and was impressed by her gift for the sport of swimming. When she walked out for meets, everyone in the crowd watched her. She was six feet tall and lean—she looked like she was made to swim. Not only was she from my home town, but she swam for the Reading YMCA, just like I did. She was also a breaststroker, which was my best stroke as well. For me, watching her race dual meet after dual meet motivated me to be viewed the same way. She was a local girl achieving amazing things in the sport, and having her so close at a time when I was improving so much made me feel like her level of success was attainable.

The summer Kristy made it to the Olympic trials for the first time, my dad and I drove out to Indiana to watch her swim. This was my first firsthand taste of Olympic-level swimming, and seeing Kristy there and being in the stands was very exciting. I know in the back of my dad's mind we made the trip so he could expose me to that meet. He wanted to plant that seed in my mind and see how I would react to it. At the time, it was just a cool meet—my goals were short term and making it to the Olympics wasn't something I'd really thought about. I was just excited to see Olympians and watch Kristy swim. I never thought I'd make it there, too.

When my freshman year finally came, I continued to train with John at Lancaster every evening until the high school swimming season started. Then when school practices started, my parents would drive me to Lancaster every morning to swim for an hour or so, and then take me to high school in time for class. This arrangement was unique—no other kids at my school got up early to practice a sport before class. The decision was mine, but it wasn't always easy. On days I didn't feel like going, my parents would remind me of the commitment I'd made and wouldn't let me skip. But I really liked working with John and wanted to stay in the water with him. The high school team practiced after school—so during that time, I spent about three hours in the pool each day. And although some high school programs have trouble getting kids to even sign up for the swim team, the Wilson team was big and very competitive. The coaches were experienced and our practices were as intense as any other practice I'd done in my career. I was fortunate to have a high school program that could help kids continue to improve if that's what they wanted.

Being a part of this team was like a dream come true for me. As the team manager the year before, I had watched my sister and Kristy Kowal swim for Wilson High, and finally being a part of that team was very exciting. The night before our first high school meet, I tried on my team suit to make sure it fit. It was a black suit with our school letters embroidered on the chest. I pulled it on and looked at myself in the mirror and felt like I was on the verge of something really great. Swimming can be a very individual sport, but when you swim for a high school team, you swim so the whole team can win. Your individual times aren't as important as the team's performance as a whole, and this made swimming much more exciting for me. And even though I was a freshman, I wanted to show everyone how well I could compete, and I wanted to motivate people the way Kristy had motivated me. I wanted to show the coaches and my fellow teammates that I was strong and a hard worker. At every practice, I pushed myself and led the lanes. Standing there in my team suit that night, with my first meet coming the next day, I was ready to make my mark on Wilson High, just like Kristy Kowal did when she swam on the team. Plus my sister, a senior that year, was on the team too. Knowing she would be there helped me relax and made me even more confident. And I was so excited about having my own Wilson team suit that I ran downstairs to show my parents.

With the swimming season underway, I could race and compete the way I always dreamed of. My passion for the sport was evident. Every time I went to the pool for practice or hung out with my teammates and friends, I felt such joy and excitement. When I swam for Lancaster and I made my Junior National cut, even though everyone on the team congratulated me, it was an individual accomplishment that didn't affect anyone on the team but me. Swimming with the high school team was much different. I can remember before one meet, everyone on the team was in the locker room changing and getting ready to go warm up. When everyone headed out to swim, my sister and a few of the other senior girls sat me down on a bench and gave me a pep talk. I was racing against a senior girl with a very good reputation in my county. She wasn't Kristy

Kowal, but she usually won her races, and I had to compete against her in the 200 IM. At that time, I was one of the strongest IM swimmers on the team, and I was in a good position to win. The senior girls told me they knew I could beat this girl, even though she was a senior. They said, "Kristen, we know you can do this. Don't be intimidated because she's a senior—you're just as fast as her."

Honestly, before they sat me down, I didn't think I'd beat her. She was four years older than me and much more experienced. I just wanted to try my best and improve my time. Even though I knew I was pretty good, I didn't give myself enough credit to beat her. But once they pumped me up, I started thinking more about the race. Her best strokes were butterfly and backstroke—the first two legs of the race. The breaststroke was the third leg, and the final one was freestyle. I knew that she'd probably be in front of me for the first few laps, and my chance to pull ahead would be during the breaststroke.

When we lined up to race, she was in lane three and I was right next to her in four. The pressure I felt at that moment was incredible. But I kept thinking about what my teammates said, and when I dove in the water, she and I were right next to each other the whole time. We were stroke for stroke—she wasn't ahead like I thought she'd be. We touched the wall at the same time and turned at the same time, even during her strongest strokes. I knew then that I could win. Then during the breaststroke, just like I thought, I started swimming faster than her. My breaststroke was stronger and I pulled ahead by a whole body length. The last stretch of the race was freestyle—not my best stroke, but good enough for me to hold on.

I touched the wall and finished the race just before her. We both looked up at our times and immediately she turned around to congratulate me. I'd swam against girls who got a little mean if they didn't win and didn't bother shaking your hand after a race. But this girl shook my hand, hugged me over the lane, and said, "Great race, Kristen." She must have been a little shocked because compared to her I was just a little freshman—she was my sister's age. But she was very gracious about it.

Before I even climbed out of the pool, all the girls on my team rushed over, pulled me out, and hugged me. My sister gave me a big hug and said, "Good job." The crowd behind us was clapping and everyone congratulated me. I was the little freshman who beat the big senior. Not only had I won my race, but my team won the meet as well.

My sister was always supportive of me, but she never pushed me. I probably pushed her more than she pushed me. I always worked really hard to lead the lanes at practice, which sometimes meant beating her. But we never experienced any sibling rivalry because she was truly a great supporter. And swimming was never her life, not the way it was mine.

Swimming, especially my freshman year at Wilson, continued to be a positive experience for me. I never let myself down—I never strived for something and didn't achieve it. And during this time I developed an intense relationship with the sport. I knew that when I was in the water I could do anything I wanted to do. And people beyond my coaches and team started noticing, too. Almost every weekend our town's newspaper mentioned my swimming accomplishments from that week's meet and even as a freshman I was starting to make a name for myself in our area's swimming community.

The last meet of my freshman year was the state championships in March. All the best swimmers in Pennsylvania were competing at the event and my parents and I traveled down to Penn State with several other swimmers from my school. I wasn't favored to win going into my race, the 100 breaststroke, and I didn't really expect to win. At that point in my career, I was still building my confidence. Then I placed second in my preliminary heat that Saturday morning and realized winning was in my reach. Going into the finals I was seeded third overall behind another freshman and a senior who had taken third in the previous year's state championship. After swimming that morning, my parents and I went out to lunch and then came back to the hotel. Although most of the girls on my team who were there with me hung out together all afternoon, my parents made me take a nap in our room so I'd be ready to race in the finals that evening. I hadn't felt my best in the water that morning and my strokes were short. Although resting all afternoon meant I'd miss out on the fun the rest of my teammates were having, I knew rest would give me the edge I needed to do better. It must have helped because I won the gold in the 100 breaststroke that evening. I was behind the other freshman for the first half of the race, but on the third lap I caught up to her and then pulled ahead for the win on the final stretch. I was the Pennsylvania state champion breaststroker—the first from my high school since Kristy Kowal!

My hometown paper ran an article about my victory and the whole team's successes at the meet. But no one was prouder of me than my dad. He wrote a letter to my school's athletic director shortly afterwards and asked if any other freshman from Wilson had ever brought home the state championship in an individual event. My parents framed the athletic director's response letter and it hung in their house for years. It read: "In response to your question regarding any ninth graders to win PIAA individual gold medals at Wilson—according to my knowledge, Kristen is the first! We hope she can keep improving and win more in the next three years."

With the high school swimming season over, I went back to my regular schedule at Lancaster. And my improvements didn't stop. That spring, I reached another big milestone in my career—I made the Senior National cut while competing at one of the Junior National meets. This was a huge accomplishment in itself, because the next step is the Olympic trials, but for me it was also significant in that I'd only made the Junior National cut six months or so beforehand. Most swimmers take a year or two to drop that much time.

Kyle, the other strong breaststroker on my Lancaster team, had also made the Senior National cut. John really wanted to see the two of us maximize our potential, and to improve your stroke, swimming lap after lap only takes you so far. After that, you have to work on other factors, like nutrition, strength, and flexibility. So John developed exercises and build contraptions for Kyle and me to use to build strength. One I remember in particular was a belt with bungee cords that attached to a board on the ground. John would have us swim a few laps, then get out of the pool and jump off the ground with this belt on. Because of the bungee cords' resistance, I could only jump up a few inches. We'd each do a set of ten jumps or so, then dive back in the water and swim a few more laps. It didn't bulk up my muscles, but I improved so much from that one simple exercise. And my legs were so sore after practices that I couldn't even sit down to go to the bathroom.

Because we were the only two on the team swimming at the Senior National level, John focused a lot of his attention on helping me and Kyle improve. Our practices were energetic and challenging, and Kyle and I always worked as hard as we could. The two of us—especially Kyle—emerged as team leaders among the other swimmers, pushing everyone at practice to accomplish their best.

Chapter 3: The Summer of Change

After swimming for Wilson High School again my sophomore year, I went back to training with John at Lancaster for the summer. Around this time I began focusing even harder on my swimming career. I had always been a hard worker, but that summer something changed in me. And with Senior Nationals coming up, I started making many sacrifices to improve. With school out, the Lancaster swim team practiced twice a day on most days of the week. And practices became much more challenging. One day at the end of practice John pulled us all out of the water and told everyone that the next day's practice would be a difficult one. He said for our main set we were going to swim 200 yards (eight laps) of our best stroke twenty times, which was such a long set of laps that most college coaches don't even make their teams practice like that. John knew the practice would be difficult for us, but he also knew the worst thing that could happen was we'd be sore the next day. And he wanted to challenge us mentally. Most coaches never tell their athletes what to expect from the next day's practice, but he'd been thinking about doing this particular set for weeks.

"We'll probably warm up, do that set, and warm down when you're done," he said. "It's your choice if you want to come or not. I'm not going to yell or get mad, but I want you to know and be mentally prepared that tomorrow is going to be a big day." John could have just as easily not said anything, and then when we all showed up the next day as usual, he could have made all of us swim the same workout.

I looked around at my teammates and we all had fear in our eyes. This would be the hardest practice of our swimming careers up to that point. Just thinking about it, I knew it was going to be painful, but I knew that I had no choice. I wanted to come to practice and give it everything I had. I looked forward to making John proud and working hard for him. Because I knew that every decision he made was in my best interest.

That night and the following day it was hard for me to focus because I knew what was coming that night at practice. Finally when I arrived at the pool, out of thirty swimmers on the team, I counted only nine that showed up to do the set—Kyle and one of my best friends, Jen, were there too. Because Kyle and I were the only two swimmers on our team to qualify for the Senior National meet, we had an incredible bond and we pushed each other at every single practice. And he was always up for the next challenge. Kyle was a very motivated and passionate person, and his passion for the swimming was contagious, so I never doubted he'd be there for the main set. Kyle pushed everyone at practice and would definitely let you know if he thought you could do better.

Kyle and I became training partners and best friends that summer—and before long he was my first boyfriend. With swimming we had an instant connection because he had also been swimming since he was just a kid. He was someone I could go to with any feeling or emotion. Having Kyle in my life made all the hard work I did at practice so much more enjoyable—and I was glad he was there with me for the main set.

Instead of John speaking negatively about those who did not make it to practice, he talked with those of us who did come and let us know how proud he was. We got in the water and had our choice of warm up for twenty minutes. Once the set started, I can remember being so scared that my stomach was in knots. But I swam in the lane next to Jen. She swam butterfly, and we pushed each other the whole time. We swam stroke for stroke the entire set, which lasted over an hour. The longest hour ever! John and a few coaching assistants timed every single lap we all swam that day, knowing this practice would help not just me and Kyle, but everyone on the whole team reach the next level.

At the end of the practice, John told everyone to cool down, then hop out of the water and gather by the bleachers. As I cooled down in the water, my heart was racing and I was exhausted. All my limbs seemed heavy and dead, but I felt a great sense of accomplishment. It was like a breakthrough. It made me think about my school friends and how I was in such a different mindset and world than they were. Most of them were probably watching TV at that moment or relaxing on the couch and they probably could not imagine challenging their bodies and minds the way my teammates and I did that night.

When all nine swimmers got together on the bleachers, John stood in front of us. He looked at each swimmer, smiled, and nodded his head. He didn't say anything for a minute or two, then when he spoke, he told us how amazing we all swam and that we should be proud of what we had just accomplished. He said he wanted us to know this was as much a mental challenge as it was a physical challenge. Because we showed up and completed this particular workout, he was confident we could do whatever we put our minds to in the future. We could be successful individuals, whether we were swimming, taking exams in college, working in a career as adults, or even the challenges that come in parenthood. John liked to challenge us mentally, not to prove to him, but to prove to ourselves we could face challenging competitions. He tried to take the anxiety out of competing, because like all sports, swimming is just as mentally challenging as it is physically. It's just swimming—it's just going back and forth in a pool. But if we were scared and didn't think we could do it, we would never swim beyond that mental barrier. If we could remove anxiety, then we could swim to our full potential. When that mental barrier is gone, it's like a weight is lifted off your shoulders and you can swim and practice even harder. Sitting on the bleachers that day, I knew this was a critical moment in my swimming career and life. It was just a couple hours in the pool, but it truly gave me pride and a confidence I could carry with me. And this was the beginning of my addiction to the satisfaction of setting and achieving goals.

The set also made me see John in much higher regard. I didn't realize it at the time, but I began to develop an unhealthy belief that every day of my swimming career would be like this; that every relationship with every coach I would ever have would feel like my relationship with John. From that point on, I never questioned anything he told me.

That summer I also started spending the night with Jen, who lived in Lancaster, so I could get an extra hour of sleep and be as rested as possible before practice. In between double practices, she and I would run three or four miles with our teammates to build up our aerobic bases. Then on Saturdays we'd practice for three hours and do dry-land workouts afterwards. My whole life revolved around swimming. But this rigorous schedule didn't bother me at all. I never felt like I was missing out on my summer vacation because I had so much fun being around other swimmers all the time. And I focused on training as hard as I could every day. Some kids on my team just pushed hard enough to get through our practices, but I worked until I was red in the face and sick. I worked one-on-one with John in the weight room to build my strength, which was a new addition to my normal training regimen. And the workouts in the weight room were intense, with numerous lunges, squat jumps, and calisthenics. That summer, I truly felt like I hit a level where I could work harder than I ever had before. It wasn't physical, but a mental barrier I broke.

John was there every step of the way. On some days he would even join the team in the weight room and participate in the workouts. This made the workouts exciting and different. And John tried to structure workouts around each swimmer's strengths and did everything in his power to help each one of us improve. He also gave us freedom to warm up and cool down however we needed. Most coaches make their teams warm up as a team with everyone doing the same exercises; but John trusted us as individual athletes to know what we needed to do to swim our best. He put all the responsibility on us.

Kyle and I shared a sort of unspoken motivation—if we were going to practice, we were going to work as hard as we could. We, especially Kyle, didn't want to be average swimmers on an average team. And we naturally emerged as leaders pushing everyone else to do their best. I enjoyed every minute of every day that summer. Although the training itself was very grueling, for some reason, I was addicted to the hard work. I could not wait to get back in the water and have a great workout. Many athletes know the feeling of after-workout bliss—the "high" or satisfaction that comes once a practice or workout is completed. I loved that feeling and I loved seeing my improvement over the weeks and months.

Although practice took up most of my time that summer, we did have fun. The swimmers went to the movies and got together at teammates' houses for dinner. But our parents were there because they were all close friends, too, so it wasn't your typical party—more like good, clean fun. At the time, I loved feeling like I was part of a big group of people who had the same interests as me.

Finally when it came time to swim the last meet of the summer, Senior Nationals in California, I was not nervous at all. I was prepared and ready—there was nothing I could have done that summer to train harder or better prepare. I was one of the slower breaststrokers to swim at the meet. Because it was my first time at Nationals, I was a young rookie competing against older veterans. Most of the girls I would race against were already in college, including Kristy Kowal. Kyle, on the other hand, was seeded higher than I was and so the focus going into the meet was more on him. I was just happy to be competing at that level.

I swam in the second heat that morning, and as I lined up at the block for my event, the 100 breaststroke, I saw Kristy Kowal lined up a few people behind me. She was seeded much higher than me, so she swam in one of the last heats of the 100. When it was time for my race, I walked up to the starting blocks, looked at John and my parents, and smiled. I knew I was ready—I had trained for months, tapered, and shaved—and could not wait to start the race. I stepped on the block, took a deep breath, and the gun went off. When I dove in the water I felt light as a feather and I swam as fast as I could. I felt like I was flying on top of the water. I had endless energy, like I could sprint the whole race. I could see, out of the corner of my eye, I was far ahead of the other girls in my heat. This meant I was going to have a great time, maybe even my personal best. Going into the meet, my goal was a time of 1:12 because that was the Olympic trials cut-off time. If I could accomplish that I might make a national team and be able to travel around the world and swim for my country.

When I finished and hit the wall, I looked up and saw 1:09.87! I won by a body length. I could not believe it. That was five seconds faster than my best time. In the sport of swimming, that is a huge improvement and drop in time. I had to look again to make sure the clock was right. Everyone in the stands was clapping and Kristy was on deck cheering for me. She gave me a big hug and told me how great I did. I was speechless—my time qualified me for Olympic trials. When I finally went over to John, he was going crazy. He had been taping the races, but he didn't get the end of mine on film because he was so excited he dropped the camera. He picked me up and screamed, "You are going to make top eight! Way to go Kris!" I was placed forty-second overall when I entered the meet. I could not fathom being one of the top eight swimmers in the country!

After all the heats in my event were finished that morning, I was in fifth place overall. Kristy Kowal was the first-place finisher. This meant that night, for the first time in my life, I was going to swim in the same heat as her. Placing fifth also guaranteed me a spot on one of the National Teams. The USA Swimming Committee selects swimmers from the top eight at Senior Nationals to swim at the Pan Pacific Championships, Pan American Games, World University Games, or Short Course World Championships. I wouldn't make the Junior National Team, which was made up of the top swimmers in the eighteen-and-under category, but I'd swim with a national team without age restrictions and the best swimmers in the country competing internationally.

I relaxed in between the morning swim and finals and went to eat with my parents and John. We called our local paper and told them about my swim—although this wasn't the first time my name appeared in print, it was my biggest accomplishment so far. It was all very exciting. After lunch, I tried to rest in my hotel room, but did not sleep a wink. I still couldn't quite grasp what I had done. In one swim, my whole career had changed. I went from being in the top 100 in the country to being the fifth best breaststroker in the United States. From that point on, I would be a recognized name in the swimming community. I knew people would expect me to continue to be one of the best at every meet. I, myself, would expect nothing less.

At finals that night I marched out to music with the fastest breaststrokers in the country: Kristy Kowal, Amanda Beard, Megan Quann, and Sticianna Stitts. John filmed the whole thing, and I was smiling from ear to ear. I enjoyed each moment and felt very relaxed—just happy to be there. I swam pretty much the same time as I did in the morning and placed fifth, qualifying for the Pan American Games Team. Pan Ams were going to be held in Winnipeg, Canada, the following year and many future Olympians would also make the meet. This was a huge accomplishment for me—one that I never expected going into the race.

I celebrated with my family, John, Kyle, and his parents that night. Kyle and I reminisced about all the hard work we both endured that summer and how we were so happy that it all paid off. By the end of the summer season I was ranked twelfth in the world in the 100-yard breaststroke. This status was both a privilege and a pain. Any USA swimmer that breaks the top fifty in the world at anytime must undergo drug testing from FINA and the USOC for the remainder of his or her career. But I felt so proud and excited about how the summer and Nationals went. This was the first time I really started to become confident in my swimming ability. A huge part of that confidence was due to my relationship with John and Kyle.

John brought out the best in my swimming talent and also the best in me as a person. Not every coach has worked with athletes competing at a national level, and he really tried to understand Kyle and I and all his other swimmers for who we were. He knew our strengths and weaknesses and helped us learn as much as we could about the sport and our bodies. He wanted us to know what we needed in and out of the water to be successful. Any coach can be lucky enough to have a naturally gifted athlete on his or her team, but if a coach can find ways to motivate that athlete beyond expectations, many times great performances happen and both the athlete and coach become very successful.

Kyle also helped me realize my potential. His energy and commitment gave me a desire to challenge and push myself to new limits. We grew really close that summer, just from training together and being on the same path. Ever since he was a little kid, Kyle had his sights set on the Olympics. When he was only ten or eleven, he sat down with his parents and John and said, "I want to go to the Olympics. What is it going to take?" So from that early age, his parents and coaches always understood what he wanted to achieve and that he was different from other swimmers. He was naturally talented, but he also had the heart required to shoot for that kind of goal.

I never really thought about the Olympics until that summer—I always tried to do my best and set goals, but I never had that ultimate goal in mind. Seeing Kyle's constant determination made me push my goals even higher.

Chapter 4: National Record!

When I started my junior year, my goal was to break the High School National Record. Kristy Kowal had set the record three years before in her senior year at Wilson, and by this time she was swimming for the Georgia Bulldogs. The record was a 1:01.47. I already had swum a 1:03.9 my sophomore year and felt like dropping two seconds was very achievable.

Throughout my junior year I continued to work hard. Three mornings a week, I made the trip to Lancaster to train with John before school. Then after school I trained with the Wilson team. Swimming with the high school team and competing in dual meets was still so much fun. All my best girlfriends were on the team—we swam relays together and traveled on the bus to different schools.

Even though I was spending more time with my high school team, John and Kyle were still a huge part of my life and I stayed in close touch with them. John felt swimming on the high school team gave me a great aerobic base, and with the sprinting he had me doing in the morning, he knew it would be the perfect combination of training I needed to break the record. Being able to believe in a coach, like I believed in John, was a great feeling. I never questioned anything he told me to do. He only did what was best for me, even if it was extremely difficult.

I wanted to shoot for the record at High School Districts—the same place Kristy set it three years before. The pool was known as a fast pool. Instead of having a shallow end and a deep end, this particular pool was about five feet deep throughout. When a pool is deeper than that, or if it has deep sections, it tends to create more drag and more waves that slow you down. The water would be ideal for me to swim my fastest.

For the couple months leading up to High School Districts, I focused on doing the little things right. For example, I did not stay out late or have sleepovers with friends. I cut out soda and fast food. I also added thirty minutes of stretching a day. John stressed that if I added stretching to my routine, it would help me tremendously. He explained that being flexible was a key factor in becoming a great breaststroker, which also requires coordination and strength. I took his word and stretched religiously. I practiced hard up until about a week and a half before the meet. Then I eased off to rest and prepare. I stretched every night and went to bed early. Before I went to sleep, I visualized the race. I imagined myself there for the meet, with the crowd surrounding the pool and the smell of chlorine and sound of the natatorium. I imagined stepping onto the block and taking a deep breath. Then I imagined the sound of the gun and diving in the water. I visualized myself swimming as fast as I could, and then touching the wall and winning. I put myself there so I would be mentally prepared and the actual event wouldn't be so intimidating. I knew I didn't want to look back on this time and think, "Well, I should have done this differently." I wanted to go in knowing I was ready.

The morning of 100-yard breaststroke at High School Districts was nerve racking. I had gotten as much sleep as I could the night before and was on the bus with my high school team bright and early. My best girlfriends were with me, and instead of chatting the whole bus ride, I told them I really couldn't talk because my mind was going a mile a minute. I put on my headphones and sat quietly in my seat. I remember looking out the bus window and thinking, "Stay calm! You are ready to do this!" Once our team arrived at the pool, I walked in the locker room and got ready to warm up. I was very quiet and kept to myself. I really needed to focus and not get distracted.

After warming up for only a couple minutes, I felt like I was ready to go. I felt extremely light and fast and could not wait any longer to swim my event. Kyle was at the meet with his high school. And because he was also swimming the 100 breaststroke, he was right near my block while

I was waiting to swim. I told him, "Please talk to me about anything but swimming right now." We had plans to go to his homecoming dance together, so just trying to make small-talk, he asked if I'd found a dress yet. Although dress shopping was truly the furthest thing from my mind, Kyle really calmed me down and let me know I was going to do great.

I looked down the pool and saw my entire Wilson High School team gathered to watch me swim. They all knew I was going after the record, and were crowded around the end of my lane, ready to cheer their hearts out for me. John had come to see me race, and he was in the stands with my parents. This was the moment I'd been working toward all year, and knowing everyone was supporting me made smiling and relaxing that much easier.

I stepped up on the blocks and took a deep breath, just like I'd practiced in my head. The gun went off and I dove in the water. That race was the only time in my life that I don't remember a single thing about how I felt. I don't remember one turn or one stroke. It was almost like my visualizations—like I was watching myself from the side of the pool. All I can remember about being in the water that day was finishing the race, hitting the wall, looking up, and seeing 1:00.74—the new High School National Record. I did it!

A rush of adrenaline came over me. I looked back to find my parents in the stands and realized everyone in the crowd was on their feet. I was getting a standing ovation from the entire pool. My team was jumping up and down in excitement. My best friends and Kyle hugged me as soon as I got out of the water. Tears of joy and extreme emotion flowed down my cheeks, and I wanted this moment to last forever. It was indescribable and something I will never forget.

Soon after setting the record, the editor of *Swimming World magazine* called my house and spoke to my dad. Swimming World is the most widely read publication that covers the sport, and I had been reading it since I was a kid. I was watching television in another room when my dad came in and said, "You were just chosen as the Swimming World High School Swimmer of the Year!"

I was so surprised. Every year the magazine chose one female and one male high school swimmer out of the entire country. I didn't have a long list of swimming accomplishments at that time, but setting the national record was a huge deal, and they literally picked me because of that one swim. I was going to have a three-page spread of photos in the magazine and also an article written about my experience—and maybe even make the cover. My parents were so proud and happy. They congratulated me and let me know they were so excited about what I had accomplished.

At this point, although I hadn't really given it much thought, my parents were thinking about where I would go for college. Bill Dorenkott, the head coach at Penn State, called my dad and started developing a friendship with him. My sister went to Penn State, and had actually been recruited to swim on the team without a scholarship. This was before Bill was there, and the other coach cut her after a few practices. But we went up to State College on the weekends for football games while my sister was there, and my parents fell in love with the school. So he was excited about Bill approaching him about me. Bill wasn't allowed to talk to me, but he went golfing with my dad and came to watch me swim at meets. Penn State, up until then, never had a very strong swim team. They never recruited swimmers on full scholarships and they weren't known as one of the top schools, like Georgia and Stanford. But Bill wanted to start building a better team and recruiting me was part of that goal. Before long, he won my parents over and they became very adamant about me going to Penn State because it was close to home and my father really felt that the coach and I would make a great match. Once his mind was made up, there was no changing it. My dad wasn't concerned about me going to a top swimming school—he had seen other student athletes leave home and eventually transfer, and he felt if I were close the pressure wouldn't be as difficult to handle. In his mind, I was too young to make such a big decision on my own. And he liked Bill and wanted me to help make a difference and build the Penn State program.

I was so focused on trials, that I didn't care that much. I wish he could have helped me make my own decision, rather than make the decision for me. His dad wasn't supportive and there for him, so he may have been overcompensating for that with me. I understood he didn't want to chance me making the wrong decision because of his protective nature. But I wish he would have trusted me to make my own decision.

I argued with them at first, saying that I wanted to make a couple trips to check out other schools, but I never got anywhere. It got to the point where I didn't feel like spending my energy on fighting with them—and finding the right school can be a difficult and time-consuming decision. I did love Penn State and really liked the coach and team. I finally decided to stop fighting my parents and gave Bill a verbal commitment to swim on his team. I still was a little bitter about not being able to take calls from other coaches or go on recruiting trips—a part of me felt like I was missing out. I would have loved to experience a couple different programs and schools. But I was so focused on swimming and improving for the Pan Ams, that it also felt kind of good to have the decision out of the way.

When school ended that summer, I moved to Orlando, Florida, to train with John. He had been offered a job coaching at a club, similar to Lancaster, and asked Kyle, Casey Coble (another swimmer from my Lancaster team), and me to come down and train with him and his new team while school was out. Kyle, Casey, and I all had big meets that summer, and being with John would help us get ready. For me, preparing for the Pan Am Games in Winnipeg was my main focus. And my parents knew training with John was critical if I wanted to keep improving. So the decision to leave Reading was a no-brainer and I moved immediately after school let out.

That summer was the most fun I had ever experienced in my life. John, Kyle, Casey, and I all shared a little apartment. I slept in one bedroom, Kyle and Casey (who were best friends) shared the other, and John slept on the couch. John's team welcomed us all, and because we were swimming at a higher level than most of the other kids, we stood out as the leaders and tried to set a good example, leading the lanes and encouraging everyone to swim their hardest. I enjoyed training and spending time with Casey, Kyle, and John. We formed a great bond that, till this day, we continue to have.

While in Florida, Kyle, Casey, and I really enjoyed not only spending time with each other, but also training with John. My training schedule stayed pretty consistent and I continued to do what helped me improve the summer before. But we were able to swim in optimal conditions. And

John gave each of us great attention and continued to teach us about swimming, our technique, and how we needed to always listen to our bodies. At this point I started to realize how lucky I was to have John as a coach. After seeing a couple different swimming programs and speaking with many other swimmers, I grew to understand not all coaches were like John. Many coaches would not put in the time and effort and attention John gave his swimmers. It was easy for coaches to go through the motions and just write workouts. And some coaches only wanted to work with high-level athletes so they could add it to their resume. But John always had our best interests in mind. He was like a father figure to us. My parents had the utmost trust in him—enough trust to send me to Florida to live with him and two other boys all summer. John was just as protective as my parents were, and I loved swimming with him. John made me want to swim well and seeing him smile and be proud of me gave me a great joy.

During my stay in Florida, *Swimming World Magazine* came to the pool where I trained and took photos of me for the Swimmer of the Year feature. They interviewed me, and John and Kyle. It was an awesome experience. Being chosen to be in the magazine and named Female High School Swimmer of the Year was a true honor. The issue would come out in August—right around the time I was competing with the USA team in Canada.

Another moment I will never forget from that summer was the day I got a call from one of the best coaches in the country, Richard Quick. He was Stanford's head coach and many swimmers he coached ended up making the Olympic team. He also coached the USA team in several Olympic Games. He called the club in Florida while I was in the water practicing and talked to John. He asked if he could talk with me about visiting Stanford (by this time, the summer after junior year, coaches are allowed to talk directly to athletes), and John, looking out for me, told him about my verbal commitment to Penn State and ended the conversation pretty quickly.

After getting off the phone, John came up to me in the pool and said, "Guess who I just talked to."

"Who?" I asked.

"Richard Quick." John told me he had called to talk to me. In the swimming world, Richard Quick is a highly respected, well known coach with an amazing track record, and if he calls to recruit you to swim for Stanford, you're pretty good. I was excited that he called me, and at the same time, disappointed that I never got to visit Stanford. But after a few minutes, I forgot about it and continued to focus on practice.

When the end of the summer rolled around, the time came for me to leave Florida for Pan American Games in Winnipeg, Canada. I was a little anxious about this new adventure. Not only would I be swimming for a national team in a faraway place, but it would also be the first time in years that I swam in a meet without John being there. My parents were coming, but the fact that John would not be on deck with me to help me warm up and talk to me made me a little uneasy. Before leaving Florida, John told me I could call him anytime and he knew I would do well. He reminded me of how hard I had worked and told me that I should really try to have some fun and enjoy the unique experience.

Once I got to Canada, I met many amazing athletes, including Kaitlan Sandeno, Ed Moses, Aaron Piersol, Beth Bodsford, Maggie Bowen, Kalyn Keller, Tim Siciliano, Dan Ketchum, Peter Marshal, and Katie Yevak, just to name a few. We all stayed in the athlete village, which was a complex of dormitories and a dining hall. Each of us picked our roommates and I was lucky enough to room with Katie, Maggie, and Beth. We had met a few months before when the whole USA team got together for a meeting in Colorado Springs, and everyone bonded really quickly because we all had such similar backgrounds and personalities. I had fun with these girls, who were all my age or a little older, and we formed a great friendship. While we were in Canada, the girls all talked about getting tattoos, the way Olympic athletes get tattooed to symbolize the event. I was too afraid to get a tattoo, but I did get my belly button pierced.

For many of the swimmers who made Pan Ams that year, it was not their first national team trip. But this was the first time I felt status, as though I was part of an elite group, and I loved it. I took a ton of pictures and had fun hanging out with the girls at the dorms. John told me before I left not to be star-struck by all the girls because I was part of that group now. I needed to see these people as peers, rather than superstars.

One of the biggest perks of being part of the USA team was all the athletic gear. They had it all laid out for us in a room of the hotel. It was unreal. Each athlete went from station to station and picked out items such as khaki pants, polo shirts, tee shirts, shorts, sweatpants, sweat shirts, bags, luggage, swim caps, and swim suits. The amount of USA apparel that we received for making the team was unbelievable. I felt so excited and still wasn't really aware of the situation I was in.

My mindset going into the meet was that I wanted to win and get my best time. But I was still very nervous about John not being there for such a big competition. At the time, I was too young to realize I should have been confident enough to swim without him there. A few hours before my race, I was warming up and saw my dad up above the pool in the balcony trying to get my attention. My mom and dad were sitting up there with Bill, who'd come to Canada to watch me. I had already given him my verbal commitment, and his presence at Pan Ams showed how excited he was about having me on the team. When I walked over to my dad, he had John on the phone—he called him because I hadn't swum well in the prelims—and he dropped the phone down from the balcony to me so I could talk to him.

"You'll be fine," John told me. "Just have fun. This is a great experience; enjoy it. You're ready to go." He didn't say anything profound or out of the ordinary—just one of his usual pep talks. But talking to him made me feel so much better. It sounds silly, but he really did relax me.

Swimming at an international competition was unlike any other meet I'd ever swum. The crowd was bigger, there were more cameras, and everyone was so excited to be there. Even though I didn't win—I got a silver medal—I swam a great time and was excited to come in second to my USA teammate, Staciana Stitts. After the event I got to stand on the blocks with my medal, and our national anthem was played because the gold medal went to an American. And by the time the August issue of *Swimming World* hit the newsstands, most everyone in the swimming community knew the name Kristen Woodring.

Chapter 5: Swimming My Best

When I started my last year in high school, I was excited about being a senior, but my mind was in a completely different place than everyone around me. My classmates were focused on social activities like senior week, prom, and weekend parties. My swim teammates were focused on weekly dual meets, districts, and state championships. And the only thing on my mind was doing everything I could to prepare for the 2000 Olympic trials the following summer. On top of all that, my three best girlfriends—Kara, Angela, and Alyssa—had graduated the year before and gone off to college, and not having them around made school less fun. So I definitely felt as though I was in my own world and somewhat of an outcast. It was hard for me to relate to my friends and teammates when the most important thing to me was making the 2000 Olympic Team.

Within the first couple weeks of school, I was confronted with a challenge. John had taken another job, this time in Arizona. At the time I was training with my high school team, but to truly be ready for trials, I needed to practice in a long-course pool for at least six months. The Olympic trials were in August and if I moved to Arizona after graduation, it would only give me a couple months of training with John. In the sport of swimming, a couple months is not enough time to accomplish the amount of work and conditioning needed to compete at such a high level. And I wanted to somehow get back to working with John, but wasn't sure how it could happen.

In talking with John and my parents, we decided we had two options: graduate early (in December) and move down to Arizona to train with John until trials, or move to Arizona immediately and finish my senior year at a high school in the area. I was not very excited about going to another high school and finishing my school career with people I did not know or grow up with. I loved Wilson and really wanted to graduate with my original class and friends. My parents and I decided if I could graduate early and move to Arizona that would be the ideal situation. That would give me six months of intense training leading up to trials with zero distractions. And I could commit to swimming and not have to worry about the stressors of school work.

We quickly scheduled an appointment with my principal to discuss the possibility of graduating early. When my parents and I went into the meeting to explain my situation, he was very understanding. The principal had been an athlete and Wilson's former high school football coach, and he understood what a unique opportunity I had to compete in trials. We told him that I had a good chance of making the Olympic Team. I was seated sixth going into the meet and the top two would qualify, and in order for me to have a chance, I needed to stick with my coach, John Pontz, who currently was coaching in Arizona. The principal agreed with no hesitation and was excited for me. He fully supported my decision to graduate early and was thrilled that I wanted to get my diploma from Wilson High School. To finish in December, I had to take one extra English course and one extra math course and I would have enough credits to graduate.

I was so happy everything was working out, and I didn't struggle at all with the additional courses. I knew early graduation would give me the singleness of purpose I needed to compete at the Olympic level, and I never thought I might miss out on something by leaving. I continued to train with my high school team, and the school year flew by. I really felt, because I set the National High School Record my junior year, I had accomplished everything I wanted to accomplish at Wilson. Kyle, who was a year ahead of me in school, had graduated that year and forfeited his freshman year at the University of Georgia until after trials, so he was already in Arizona with John training. And I knew I made the right decision to head out there as well. As the months progressed and my graduation date grew closer, the reality of my situation began to set in. School would be over for me and my life was going to change, but my classmates would still be going through the same routine. I got more and more excited by the day—I was mentally and physically ready to start training. Every day that passed brought me one step closer.

We decided my mother and I would rent an apartment close to the pool where I would be training. My father wanted to join us, but was unable to leave his job. He asked for a leave of absence, but his company wouldn't give it to him. Although this seemed like a setback at first, it actually was a blessing because my father decided to leave his job and start his own business. This gave him the freedom to come out and visit my mother and me once a month.

At the end of the fall semester, some of my classmates threw me a going-away party. Then a couple days after Christmas, I took a flight down to Arizona and my mom and dad drove. We needed to have a car there, so they both decided take a couple days and make the trip. As soon as I landed, I found Kyle and John in the airport waiting for me. Seeing them made me realize how much I loved being around them. We all had such a close bond that we were like family. They lived together in Arizona with another roommate and I had to stay with them for a couple nights until my parents arrived. I really felt like I was in my comfort zone. My training was going to be difficult—definitely a step up from what I'd ever done before—but I was looking forward to it. During the first couple days in Arizona, I was so happy and excited to be there. Most girls my age were consumed with school work, picking a college, and their social lives. I, on the other hand, was so focused on my training and working hard every day to prepare for the most competitive swimming meet in the world that I did not have a single regret about moving and leaving my friends and family. I felt so privileged to be in my situation and I planned on enjoying every minute.

Six days a week my alarm clock went off at 4:30 a.m. Kyle came to pick me up when it was still dark outside and we were in the pool by 5:30. John didn't want us to train in the intense heat of the day—the heat can drain the body of energy and therefore our workouts would suffer—so we scheduled our practices around the sun. We would practice in the morning from 5:30 to 7:30 a.m. After that we would have an hour-long dry-land workout consisting of medicine balls, squat jumps, walking lunges, stretch cords, and flexibly work. After practice I'd go back to our apartment and my mom and I would eat lunch and relax by the pool. We might do something fun, like go to the mall, but most of the time between practices I spent resting and mentally preparing for my next workout. Then our second water workout was from 6:00 to 8:00 p.m., after the sun went down. While training in Arizona, John and Kyle taught me many things about the sport of swimming. John was an amazing coach during that time period. He really listened to what Kyle and I had to say and therefore we both trained in the best conditions possible.

Shortly after moving to Arizona, John suggested Kyle and I start taking creatine and some other protein supplements to help our bodies recover from the intense work we were doing. I think he knew some of our competitors were taking it to help recover and gain strength, and it seemed like something that might help us as well. So after working out, I mixed the powder with grape juice. I looked at it as a step up from a protein bar, which was what I usually ate after a workout to help my body recover. And although it didn't taste very good, I was willing to try anything that might help. That's what I was there for, to do whatever it took to improve.

Although the creatine seemed to work well for Kyle—he gained strength and recovered quickly from muscle soreness after intense workouts—I started gaining weight and it actually hurt my performances. My weight had always been steady at about 133 or 134 pounds, and my body fat percentage was low. After only a few weeks of taking the creatine, I gained about seven pounds. I felt bloated and heavy, my clothes got tight, and the weight showed in my face and shoulders. I can remember looking in the mirror and feeling self-conscious about my weight for the first time. I didn't get a belly or anything like that, but I was bulkier than I'd ever been before. On Super Bowl Sunday that year, I can remember being at a party with the swim team and not wanting to eat pizza because I had already gained so much. This challenge was completely new to me—I'd always been able to eat whatever I wanted and never gain an ounce. And instead of feeling light and fast in the water, I felt heavy. My swimming suffered too. I competed in small meets while living in Arizona and my times were not improving.

The weight gain was obvious to everyone around me as well. I wore a bathing suit every day, and so I couldn't hide much. John finally sat me down to talk with my about my weight gain—certainly a delicate subject to breach with a teenage girl. But he could not have been more sensitive. He started by asking me how I liked the creatine and how I felt it was working. He knew weight issues for girls were a serious subject and he made sure to let me know he was concerned solely about my performance. He said that at this point in time, gaining weight was the last thing I needed. I should be as lean as possible if I wanted to swim my best. He and I were on the same page and we both knew that for me to be where I wanted to be at trials, I needed to slim back down. I was really frustrated at the time because I felt like the weight gain put me back a step. My confidence started slipping and I started questioning whether I'd be able to compete in trials. And I'd never had to lose weight before so I didn't know what to expect. Stopping the creatine supplements was the first step.

My parents, who had noticed the weight gain as well, also agreed that we needed to do something and were willing to do whatever it took to help me lose the weight. My dad was there visiting my mom and me that weekend, and I think seeing me with so much extra weight triggered something in my dad that made him want to fix the situation. He's always been a weight-conscious person and he didn't want anything to compromise my swimming, and so he made an appointment for me with the Diet Center of Arizona, a weight loss clinic that was near our apartment, for the following Monday morning. To be honest, I was looking forward to going to the diet center. I don't think I could have lost the weight on my own because I'd never had a nutritionist or anyone to tell me how to make the best food choices. I knew the difference between healthy food and junk food, but I didn't know what it took to lose weight. As an athlete, I'd always been interested in anything that could help me improve, and I was excited to learn more about nutrition.

Monday morning my mom and I went to the appointment. A dietician weighed me, took my body fat percentage (21 percent), and my measurements. She then gave me tools to lose the weight in a healthy manner. I was to keep a food diary of everything I ate during the day, and completely cut out dairy and heavy starchy foods, such as pizza, pasta, and breads, for the first two weeks. I had never been a salad person before, but on my new diet I had to eat plenty of fruits, vegetables, and salads. This drastic change, the dietician said, would jump start my weight loss and get me moving in the right direction. Although I had probably eaten chicken wings for dinner the night before, I implemented her suggestions right away. It was a huge change, but I was good about it and didn't cheat.

Going through the diet center program gave me great knowledge about health and nutrition. I did not think I was fat; but I truly knew my body fat percentage needed to drop if I wanted to swim my best at trials. My mother was a huge help in changing my diet. She cooked every meal for me and followed the standards I needed to abide by. That made it very easy to lose the weight, and within six weeks, my body fat dropped to 13 percent and I was in the best shape of my life.

With my weight back to normal, I started to make great strides in training and my times continued to drop. About eight weeks before trials, I was competing with the swim team at an invitational meet and I broke the Arizona state record in the 100-meter breaststroke. I was swimming faster than ever, and after such a big setback, this boosted my confidence. It was a sign that all my effort was working and I knew I was ready for trials.

When August rolled around, Kyle and I could not have been more mentally and physically prepared to race. We trained faster in the water than ever before, our dry-land routine was intense, and our nutrition program was near perfect. John was on top of everything—he did everything he could to prepare us to swim in the Olympic Trial setting. Trials were going to be held in Indianapolis—the same pool me and my dad had traveled to four years before to watch Kristy Kowal swim. John knew this pool was deep and had hard, flat walls, so he built a replica wall to put in our practice pool in Arizona so we could turn on it. And we knew if we swam well at trials, we'd be swimming up to three times in two days in the preliminary, semi-final, and final races. Prelims would be in the morning and semi-finals would be in the evening of the same day, and then we'd have less than twenty-four hours to prepare for finals if we made it that far. This would be a challenging meet for us, especially having never gone to trials before. John knew this could affect our performance and made us practice the same scenario with such a short time between intense swims. Three races in two days would be mentally challenging for me because I couldn't back off on prelims and semi-finals to save my energy for the finals. Although some swimmers, like Michael Phelps, can do that because they're confident they'll get to the finals, I wasn't seeded high enough and I knew I had to swim my hardest in all three races to make it to the next round.

John, Kyle, and I all flew to Indianapolis together, and we were all excited about having the opportunity to go to such a big event and see all the past Olympians compete. For Kyle, trials brought him one step closer to his lifelong goal, and I was more nervous for his race than I was for my own. I knew that my chances of making the Olympic Team were pretty slim—only the top two in each event make it. But after swimming a 1:09 and setting the record in Arizona, I thought I might be able to sneak in there and make second. Even if I didn't make the team, I wanted to swim my best time and see as many great athletes compete as possible. Kristy Kowal, Megan Quann, and Staciana Stitts were going to be there. And Kyle was one of the favored swimmers to win his race, so I was excited about possibly seeing him make the team.

When I got to Indianapolis, my parents and grandparents were all there to see me swim. And I found out that Kara, Angela, and Alyssa had also made the trip to watch me. As I was warming up the first morning of races, I was standing on the side of the pool and the girls were up in the stands. The first thing they said to me was, "Oh my god! You look so skinny!" They were so funny and comforting—they could care less if I was a good swimmer, they were just happy to see me after all those months.

When it came time to swim in the preliminary 100-meter breaststroke event, I still wasn't nervous. I swam my hardest—1:09.37, almost my best time—and placed fifth. When I hopped out of the pool, I was happy with my performance. But as I was getting ready for semi-finals that evening, I looked around me at all the other girls there and realized I was competing against swimmers who were in a different league. These girls were faster and more experienced than me—some of them were swimming 1:08, a whole second faster than my best time. All the nerves went away because I knew I wasn't going to drop two seconds and place first or second. Every nerve and thought I'd built up about the event left my head and it felt like any other meet. I knew I would probably make the top eight and I wasn't preparing myself to lose, but in my heart, I knew making the top two would be out of reach. To make the team I would have to go at least a 1:07.9 and that was too much of a drop. I still swam my hardest in semi-finals that evening and placed sixth with a 1:09.78.

I was so happy to make the finals and get to race against the best swimmers in the country. Knowing I probably wouldn't make the team helped me relax a little and I was able to enjoy the experience of being there a little more than some of the athletes who knew they were close and felt pressure to make it. My family and friends were there, and having the people I loved watch me swim motivated me a great deal. I wanted to swim my heart out and really give them something to be proud of.

In the ready room before finals the next morning, some girls were listening to music and keeping to themselves. Others were goofing off and very relaxed. Kristy Kowal was in there with me, and we small-talked for a few minutes about our families, which was a comforting way to keep my mind off what was coming next. She had been to the 1996 Olympic trials four years before, so she knew what to expect swimming in the finals. But she might have been under a little more pressure to perform than I was that day because she placed third the last time and just missed making the team.

When the announcer called our event, the women's 100-meter breaststroke, the eight of us—the best breaststrokers in the country—lined up to march out to the pool deck. We heard the music start outside the ready room and out we went. Everyone in the stands was on their feet and cheering. The music was blasting and energy filled the arena. I looked up and spotted my parents and friends holding signs that read, "Go Kris!" It was unbelievable, and I can remember being so present and enjoying every moment. I smiled and waved to the crowd. When we reached our lanes, the announcer went one by one and called out each girl's name. I could not believe I was finally living the moment I waited over a year for. So many feelings, emotions, and sacrifices led me to that place.

Then the gun sounded and the race was off. I swam as fast as I could for two laps and managed to place fifth with a time of 1:09.51—not top two, but still a great showing. All three swims of mine were really close in time, so I knew I got everything out of myself that I could have possibly gotten. I peaked there, but at the time I didn't think twice about it. It was a solid performance and my emotions were leveled and content.

John and Kyle came up to congratulate me. I warmed down oblivious to what I had just accomplished—I was the fifth fastest breaststroker in the country. I would not realize how great of an accomplishment the 2000 Olympic trials really were for me until a couple years later. At the time I think I was so focused on my race and watching Kyle, that I never sat back to comprehend how close I came to making the Olympic Team, which was why I had graduated early and trained for all those months. I wasn't disappointed that I didn't make the team because I knew I had trained my hardest and done everything I could do to swim my best. And with Kyle's event, the 200-meter breaststroke, coming up, I shifted my focus to watching him.

Kyle was ready to swim and extremely confident. He made it to the final heat and was seated third going into the race. I remember him telling me that if he was close to the lead at the last turn, then the race was over. He was going to find a way to win and make the team. Kyle's last fifty meters were always the fastest in the field and he knew he would win if he was close to the leader on the last turn.

John and I could not have been more nervous. I knew all the sacrifices Kyle had made and how much he wanted to make the team, so I was definitely more nervous for his race than I was for mine. When his race started, I was standing right behind his lane on the pool deck. On the first few laps he was right next to Ed Moses, Tom Wilkins, and Brendan Hansen. At the last turn, the four of them were dead even. My heart was racing and I was screaming. I knew when they made that turn he was going to win. As Kyle swam towards me, he slowly increased his lead. It was an indescribable moment. All the hard work, long practices, sweat, and tears came down to this second. When he touched the wall, John, Kyle, and I all looked up at the score board . . . first place! Kyle was going to Sydney, Australia, to swim in the 2000 Olympic Games!

As soon as he got out of the water, Kyle was whisked away for interviews and drug testing, and I started preparing for my next challenge: starting my freshman year at Penn State.

Chapter 6: Super Star?

The day after Olympic trials, I got on a plane and flew to Penn State. I didn't go home because I had to be on campus to check in my dorm and start class, and although I didn't realize it at the time, I was leaving the people who I was most comfortable with: John and Kyle.

John went back to Arizona to work and Kyle went to Georgia to start school. But the three of us left each other knowing we'd stay in touch. When I hugged John to say goodbye, I was really upset. But he said it was no big deal. "You'll be fine, Kris," he told me. "I'll talk to you next week."

Leaving Kyle was difficult, not only because we were best friends and training partners, but he'd been my boyfriend for three years. We were still dating and at the time we thought we'd be together forever, despite the long distance between us. He wanted me to come to Georgia with him because he wanted me to be close and because the swimming program had such a high reputation—Kristy Kowal, as well as several other Olympians, had gone to Georgia. The athlete in him wanted me to be a part of the best program possible, and he had a hard time accepting that I was going to Penn State. The fact that he'd had the chance to visit several schools and choose his favorite bothered me a little, but I didn't want to argue with my parents. Plus I trusted my dad's opinion of the coach and Penn State team. And working with John had left me with the confidence to believe I could keep improving no matter what.

When I arrived at State College, I was excited about meeting new people and starting this new phase in my life. Although I was a little nervous about going back to school and attending class, I quickly found out that athletes on scholarship are treated pretty well. Instead of searching through bookstores and comparing prices, all my books were ready and paid for when I picked them up. My roommate was another swimmer, Becky, who I'd swum with at the Reading Y as a kid. I knew she was going to Penn State and I requested her as my roommate. Our parents helped us move into our room and bunk our beds. And all the other students in our dorm were freshmen athletes as well.

After setting the high school record with 1:00:74, I wanted to try to break a minute in college. I'd be swimming in a short course again, like I did in high school, and I was in such good shape from training for trials that I knew dropping a second from my time was within reach. The first dual meet, a home meet against Purdue, I set a pool and a school record in both the 100 and 200 breaststroke events. I had swum well in practice and had unofficially clocked a 1:02, which would have broken the record. So I had a good feeling I'd do it again at the meet. It was still very exciting and I can remember calling John afterwards to tell him about the record. The 100-yard was less a surprise than the 200-yard, which was never my best event. John was shocked. Swimming times are never usually that good so early in the season because most athletes are still exhausted from training. And my 200 time dropped about four seconds, which is a huge improvement. Plus, I was always a sprinter; the longer 200 races exhausted me and the only reason I swam that event against Purdue was because I was a breaststroker. John asked me why I thought I had swum so fast, and at the time I didn't really give it much thought. Looking back I realize I was still in such good shape from training long course in Arizona that racing short course was a piece of cake. John probably knew this was why I did so well—all I knew was I felt really good.

Although I'd been to international meets and Olympic trials, I truly enjoyed swimming in the college atmosphere and competing against

Big Ten schools. I also enjoyed training with a large team rather than with a couple people, like I did prior to college. When I set the record, everyone—even the guys on the team—congratulated me and I felt really accepted. Being part of a big team was fun, and our coach, Bill Dorenkott, planned activities to bring the team together. Every year the whole swim team traveled to Florida over winter break to train outside in the warm weather. Rather than flying everyone down on a plane, we all rode together on a tour bus with television screens and a bathroom in the back. Bill said that it would toughen us all up—if we could swim fast after a twenty-four-hour bus ride, then we could handle any travel challenge that came our way. It definitely helped the team moral. The girls had so much fun singing, joking, and trying to find the most comfortable spot to sleep.

Bill was a different kind of coach than John. I knew the minute I met John that I liked him because he was so friendly and easy to approach. Bill was all business. He had moments when he'd loosen up and joke around with us, but they were rare. I knew he appreciated me and the other girls in my freshman class. One other girl, Corrie, and I were the first female swimmers recruited by Penn State to get full scholarships, and one of the reasons we were there was to help build the team.

After our training trip to Florida, we came back to train for a month to get ready for the Big Ten Championship meet. This meet was unlike any other I'd ever swum at. Everything was more team oriented, with all the parents wearing school colors and sitting together in the stands. Every parent cheered for every swimmer on the team, rather than just focusing on their own kids. And none of the swimmers talked to swimmers from other schools. Although being part of the team was one of the reasons I liked swimming so much in the beginning, in recent years it had become a very individual sport for me. It felt good to be part of something bigger again. At Big Tens, every race added points to the team's overall score, so even if I didn't win or make a personal best time, the team still got points from my performance. And the energy at the meet was so intense that swimmers who weren't expected to do well often did because of all the excitement. It's not hard to get a best time at Big Tens.

Penn State never placed well at Big Tens—they were usually at the bottom of the division. But as a team, everyone was swimming well and placing high, putting our team in a position they'd never been in before. We set numerous personal best records and both medley relays set team and Big Ten records. Penn State ended up placing second. I swam the best time of my life and was the first female from the Big Ten to break a minute in the 100-yard breaststroke with a 59.77. Not only did this accomplish my goal, but I was also named Big Ten Freshman of the Year. This was such a huge accomplishment for me that I wanted to reach even higher: NCAA champion.

Shortly after Big Tens, the distance became too difficult and Kyle and I decided to take a break. I had been to Georgia to visit him once, but by that point we had both found new friends and started new lives at school. I had also stopped talking to John as much. I felt comfortable with my new coach and team, and although I missed him sometimes, I didn't feel like I needed John to still swim well. Plus he was busy coaching the swimmers on his own team, and I had to focus on swimming my best at NCAAs.

The only other swimmer to break a minute that year was Tara Kirk, a swimmer from Stanford. She and I swam close to the same times all year, and heading into NCAAs, I was seeded second behind her. If I could just break a minute again and better my time by a couple tenths, I could win.

Ten other swimmers from the Penn State girls' team made it to the NCAA Championships, and so we all trained together for the weeks leading up to the event. When the time came for NCAAs, I was mentally and physically ready. Hard work and training never bothered me, and I enjoyed every part of the process leading up to the meet. Training with the small group and making the trip to Texas together was so much fun.

Our 200 medley was my first race and we had a great swim. We placed seventh overall, which was another PSU record, and I had my fastest split of my life, 59.48. This time gave me great confidence going into the 100-yard breaststroke. After the prelim swim in the morning, I was still seeded second going into the final race that night. Tara Kirk was seeded first. Tara and I swam against each other at the 2000 Olympic trials. She placed tenth and I placed fifth, so I had beaten her before and I knew I could do it again. When I was sitting in the ready room that night, I had a mix of nerves and excitement, but my adrenaline was definitely pumping.

Just before walking out, Tara came over to me and asked, "Are you Kristen Woodring?" I answered her and then she said something I will never forget: "Let's go out there and show them what breaking a minute looks like!" This was an unbelievable moment in my swimming career. I looked up to Tara very much and respected her as a fellow athlete. For her to approach me at all was very motivating, but her energy that night gave me such a jolt of readiness. I could not wait another minute to race.

After marching out and waving to my parents, teammates, and coaches, I took my place behind the block. When the gun went off, the eight of us dove in the water. During the race, I felt awesome in the water. I can remember pushing hard to keep my pace by hitting every turn and pull out. When I hit the wall and the race was over, I looked up to see my time and place and saw: third and 59.96.

Third—I was third at NCAA Championships, a First Team All-American as a freshman. And everything that I accomplished was huge for my school—no swimmer at Penn State had ever competed the way I did that year. But yet I was disappointed. Seeing that the second-place swimmer, Ashley Roby, swam a 59:91, and the winner, Tara Kirk, swam a 59.18, I knew I could have and should have swum faster.

My sister, Angela and I summer team photo. 1992.

Freshman Year at Wilson High School.

Lancaster Aquatic Club... Jenn and I after practice.

Angela, Alyssa, Kara and I. My Junior Year at Wilson.

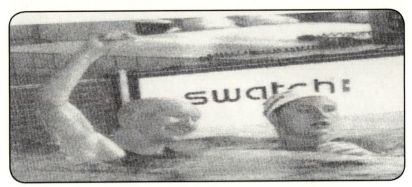

1999 Pan American Games...winning the silver medal in the 100 meter breaststroke.

My last high school swim meet before moving to Arizona to train for the Olympic Trials.

Article written in local paper about Trials.

2002 Big Ten Championships...getting ready to race.

2005 Big Ten Women's Swimming and Diving Champions.

Mom, Me, Angela, and Dad Christmas 2007.

Chapter 7: Sinking

After my freshman year, I trained all summer with the Penn State team. One of the freshmen girls coming into the program that year was from my hometown area. Her name was Courtney and she was a breaststroker like me, so we were always sharing lanes and practicing together. We started to build a strong friendship and after a couple weeks she told me that when she was younger, she remembered swimming against me at meets. Getting to know me, she said, was so great because she always looked up to my swimming accomplishments. She didn't expect me to be as down to earth and friendly as I was.

Despite making new friends, when school started back up again, my feelings about swimming and the program began to change. I felt different in the water, and I started to question whether or not Penn State was the best place for me. The biggest issue was that my stroke started slipping and I felt like I should have gotten more technical support, like what I had with John back in high school. John used to video-tape me during practices and give constant attention to my stroke to prevent bad habits from forming. Also, when the swimming conditions weren't optimal, such as water temperatures or illness, we did not train. If the temperature of the water was too hot or too cold, John had us workout on land with the medicine ball or stretch cords, or we would watch films of Olympic swimmers and try to learn from the greats. If we were sick, he would send us home to get healthy before getting back into the water. John didn't believe in "garbage yardage" (doing lap after lap at a slow speed) and mindless swimming. He had Kyle and I learn about swimming and become very knowledgeable about the technicalities of breaststroke. I eventually learned how to make corrections to my stroke when I needed to, but when I got in the water sophomore year, I felt myself getting slower and I didn't know how to correct my mistakes.

I was still training at a high level, but being a breaststroker, technique was a huge factor. Breaststroke is the most difficult swimming stroke to learn and to do. The movements are very unnatural and strain the knees and joints. The stroke is based more on flexibility and coordination, than just pure strength and endurance. I missed that consistent fine-tuning that I got in the past with John. And when my stroke started slipping that year, not one of my coaches tried to correct it. They had sixty swimmers and couldn't focus or specialize on one athlete or the other. They never taped us or showed us how to correct our strokes, and I started to realize how lucky I was to have John as my coach in high school. Because I was so used to getting individual attention and having the technical details of my stroke checked all the time, I started resenting my coaches at Penn State and my father for insisting I went there.

I continued on with practice and dual meets without voicing my problems, but I did not have a great dual meet season as I did the previous year. In the middle of the season, the team traveled to Chicago to swim against Northwestern. My parents made the trip to watch me, and I remember swimming the 200 event and placing fifth. My time was seconds above what it should have been and even though the 200 was never my best event, I usually won or placed second every time I swam it. I just didn't feel as smooth in the water as I had before, and when I got out I had this feeling in the pit of my stomach that I'd never experienced before. I wanted to go into the locker room and never come out—I was so embarrassed. This was the first time I had trouble dealing with a loss—this was the first time it really upset me. After breaking all those records freshman year, I felt like everyone had such high hopes for me. And placing fifth in a dual meet was heading in the complete opposite direction.

My parents definitely noticed my poor performance. We went out for dinner afterwards and I couldn't stop crying. My dad kept saying, "Don't worry about it; it's not that big a deal." I was crying harder than I'd ever cried about a race and they didn't understand why. They didn't understand how I felt inside. To them, it was just another race. All I remember saying was that I had tried my best. Usually, though, when I tried my best I won. Winning had always come so easy, and at nineteen years old, I couldn't handle defeat.

Instead of being positive and looking for a solution, I became this negative, difficult person to be around. As my times increased, my attitude toward swimming and the coaches got worse and worse. Bill never approached me about my performances slipping—never offered any tips for improving. He was in and out of practice, always busy with recruiting or other business. Even though I never approached Bill with my problems, I resented him for not noticing. John had always noticed—he was always on top of it, making sure I was doing what I was supposed to be doing. For this reason, I always trusted John, and I found it difficult to trust Bill and his different coaching style. The combination of my stroke falling apart, my negative attitude, and the fact that John wasn't there to help me created a big mess. My resentment and negativity began to overpower me so much that even if Bill would have offered some help, I probably would have rebelled against it. Looking back, Bill didn't coach me any different sophomore year than he did freshman year. But not getting stroke attention and support freshman year didn't matter to me because I was swimming so well. Something inside me had changed—I had never rebelled against authority before. I had always been a leader, a good example on the team.

When I brought my feelings up with my parents, they both sort of blew it off, saying, "Oh, you'll be fine. Just keep going." They thought I was just being negative and didn't want to delve into it. As the season went on, my negativity swelled so much it was impossible not to notice. In the locker room, instead of being a positive, upbeat role model for the other girls, they all heard me cussing the coaches and the program, and saying things like, "This sucks," and, "This doesn't work." For someone who had always been seen as a leader, this was the worst thing I could do for the team morale.

A few weeks before Big Tens, we were doing a medicine ball workout on the pool deck and I was purposely slacking off. My partner would throw the ball to me, and I made a visible effort to not take it seriously. I slouched and barely put my strength behind my throw when I sent it back to her. Finally Bill stopped me. He paired my partner with someone else and pulled me aside.

"What's your deal, Kristen?" he said.

"I just don't feel like doing this," I said. My eyes started to sting with tears when I looked at him.

"You realize that people on this team look up to you, so stop goofing off."

This was the first time Bill confronted me about my behavior. But at that point, I think I was too far gone to pull myself out. When he said these things to me, I felt torn. I knew deep down that coaches are there to help and support athletes, but at the time I felt like Bill saw me as a number, not an individual. Instead of seeing I was upset and helping me because he cared, I felt like Bill just wanted me to get better so I could swim faster. If they really cared, they would have given me time off. I didn't realize the feelings I was experiencing were tell-tale signs of depression.

Everyone saw what was happening to me. Courtney especially noticed the transformation. She saw me lash out and be difficult at practice, and then when we hung out in the dorm together or went to the movies, she also saw how sad I was, crying at night for no apparent reason and feeling depressed about swimming. I think she knew there was more to it than what was visible on the surface, and when she confronted me about it, I just blamed it on the coach or the program. "This isn't what I need," I told her. "This wouldn't be happening if I were swimming somewhere else."

Looking back, this was such a terrible thing to say to any teammate—let alone the one that looked up to me the most. I'm sure most of the girls on the team didn't know what to say to me. But I could see in their body language at practice and in the locker room that my behavior made them uncomfortable.

Once Big Ten Championships came around, my self confidence was at an all time low. I had withdrawn from almost everyone on the team. Courtney sat with me on the bus, but I rode almost the whole way with my headphones on, staring out the window. I withdrew from my teammates because I had never felt so down on myself in my life. Although my poor times sparked these feelings, I also felt crazy for the way I was acting. It seemed so silly—it was only swimming—but I became so unconfident and anxious about everything.

I was still seated first going into the Big Ten meet, but instead of going for a personal best time, all I wanted was to hold on for a win. Freshman year, and every year in high school, winning seemed like an afterthought. I was more concerned with beating my personal best times, rather than winning heats. Now, it was the complete opposite. I felt that all of my competitors were breathing down my neck and I had no adrenaline or drive for swimming and racing like I did in the past. Instead of being excited to race, win, and set records, I was anxious and nervous about what the outcome might be. I knew based on my times that I could beat the other girls, but I had all these doubts in my mind. I started thinking about disappointing my parents and not living up to everyone's expectations. Instead of enjoying the experience of going to the conference championship with my teammates, I just wanted to get my races over with and get out of the water.

During my race, I felt like I was wading through mud instead of gliding through the water. I was ahead, but only by a little. And at every turn, I saw the girl right behind me. Situations like this used to motivate me to push harder, but during this race it scared me. I really had to push myself to get my hands on the wall, and when I finished and looked at the girl who had been right behind me, I couldn't tell if I beat her or not. She had already touched and come up too. When I looked and saw "first place" next to my name on the board, I thought, "Thank God." My time was over two seconds too high, but all I cared about was that number one next to my name.

I won by 2/100 of a second. My teammates, Courtney and Lindsey, placed third and fifth, and I was happier for them than I was for myself. I congratulated the girls and went to the locker room to sob. An overwhelming feeling of sadness came over me, and I could not get past the fact that I increased my time from 59.77 to 1:01.15. Instead of enjoying the fact that I was a Big Ten Champion, two years in a row, I felt awful. I wanted so badly to compete at a high level that seeing this increase in time made me sick to my stomach. I could not understand what went wrong. Up until this point, I had always been able to train hard, rest, and drop time. I felt so uncomfortable in my own skin and I didn't know how to make myself feel better. After the race I was supposed to meet my parents in the stands so we could go out for dinner, but I dreaded having to see them. I knew they would be mad about my behavior and my time.

Two weeks later I was back at NCAAs, this time with a totally different attitude. I was negative about everything, and I disagreed with everything my coach said to me. When it came time for my races, I thought that I was trying my best, but I was not. There was no way I could have been—I had no desire to compete, and it showed in my performances. I did not make a final in any of my events. I did make the consolation heat in the 100-yard breaststroke, which meant I got to swim again at night, but not in the final race with the top eight. Anyone would have been proud of this accomplishment, but for me it was kind of embarrassing because I had placed third the year before.

Every day of the meet, I cried and moped around. Even though none of the swimmers from Penn State made it to the finals, we all stayed to watch the races. So I sat on deck while the top eight marched out for the final race and I felt so jealous of all the girls that I had swum with last year. Tara Kirk, who had won the year before, won again. Seeing her, and even the new girls who had made it to the top eight for the first time, made me miss that feeling of pride and excitement.

On the last day I was sitting alone with tears streaming down my face. I was near the team, but with my back turned, because I was too ashamed to show my emotions to the girls. I saw my coach walking towards me and, thinking he was approaching me to talk to me about what was going on, I felt a slight sense of calm. Even though I had been fighting with him and being a difficult athlete to coach, I so badly wanted someone to sit and talk with me. Not necessarily about how I swam at the meet, but simply someone to talk with. As my coach approached me, I kept my head down, still embarrassed of how I looked. And in a split second, I realized he walked right past me and continued down the pool deck. He wasn't approaching me at all. This only fueled my frustration and anger. Later I found out, from my teammate Sally, that when Bill walked by, he turned, looked down at me, and kept on walking.

My dad, on the other hand, did say something to me. Right in the middle of the lobby, surrounded by other swimmers and their coaches and families, my father threw a fit because I was crying after each race and not taking advantage of the opportunity to swim at NCAA Championships. It happened right after my 100-yard consolation heat and I was still a mess about placing twelfth. He said, "You're being ridiculous! I don't want to see you crying anymore! You're at the fastest meet in the country and you're acting like a big baby!"

This was the first time I ever told my parents: "I do not want to swim!" But it didn't seem to affect him the way I thought it would. My dad loved me more than anything, and always wanted me to have every opportunity, but when he saw me acting the way I was at NCAAs, he just couldn't stand it. I continued to tell my parents how unhappy I was and that I did not enjoy swimming anymore, and they told me it was just a phase I was going through and that I would get over it.

After NCAAs, the usual procedure was for all the swimmers to take two weeks off and then come back to start spring training. Not me. The Phillips 66 National Championships were less than two weeks away and after NCAAs, Bill told me and Corrie Clark, my teammate who was recruited the same year I was, that he'd see us at practice on Monday. He knew they were picking swimmers at nationals to represent the USA at four different meets: Pan Pacific Games, Pan American Games, World University Games, and Short Course World Championships. Most athletes would be thrilled to have an opportunity like this. At the time, swimming was the last thing that I wanted to do, let alone train hard and focus on making a national team. I wanted to relax and take a breather from everything. I did not have the correct mindset to prepare physically, mentally, and emotionally for nationals. But not going was never considered an option. Based on our past performances, Corrie and I had a good chance of making a team, which would look really good for Penn State. So I had to keep going.

At nationals, I placed tenth. My time was two or three seconds higher than what I swam at Olympic trials, so it wasn't my best, but placing tenth was pretty good. It wasn't good enough to make a national team, though, because only the top eight make it. So I was relieved that I would finally have a break from swimming. I was not too disappointed, to say the least. Corrie, on the other hand, did swim very well and ended up making The World University Games team. I was thrilled for her. She worked really hard all year and she deserved it.

As I was heading for the locker room, though, Bill and Corrie approached me with some news. Bill told me that a couple people from the top eight in my event declined the invitation to go on one of the national trips, which meant I was bumped up and made The World University Games team with Corrie. We were going to travel to China together. They were both smiling at me and so excited about our good luck. And I smiled and said, "That's awesome." But inside my heart sank. I did not have any drive or passion left to swim. Being an athlete is almost impossible if there is nothing inside driving you to continue.

After hearing the news I was numb with disappointment. I changed in the locker room and then went to meet my parents at the car. When I got in the back seat and told them that I made the World University Games team, I lost it. All my emotions rushed out and I started to bawl. I had been crying a lot those days, but usually quietly to myself. This time I was sobbing. I told my parents that I just wanted to go home. I told them I did not want to go to China; I wanted to take some time off. This was not an option.

"Absolutely not," my dad told me. "You know everyone is so excited for you, Kristen."

When I tell this story to people now, they always ask why I didn't just refuse to go. Honestly, this never crossed my mind—especially after my parents were so adamant about me going. When it really came down to it, I trusted that they would make the best decision for me. This was the first time any swimmers from Penn State were going to represent the United States in an international meet, and it was huge for the school. All the papers wrote about it and with so much attention on our accomplishment, swimming in China wasn't just about me anymore. On the surface it looked like I was swimming well and doing great things. But inside, I was freaking out. My parents felt that I was acting selfish and not appreciating my talent. On the outside I absolutely looked that way, but my intentions were not to be selfish. I just needed time to think and figure out what was going on with me.

That summer I trained to compete at the World University Games in Beijing. A couple weeks into training, a photographer came to my practice and asked if he could take a few pictures of me. When I asked what they were for, he informed me that I had been chosen to be painted on "The Mural of Inspiration," which was being painted on a wall in downtown State College. I immediately knew what he was talking about—the painting across from my parents' favorite restaurant, a place called The Deli—and I could not believe it. He let me know that only two athletes were chosen for the entire mural, one male and one female. The male was Adam Taliaferro, a football player who injured his spinal cord during a Penn State game and became paralyzed. He worked very hard in rehab and miraculously regained the ability to walk against the doctors' predictions.

I was very flattered to be the female athlete in the mural with so many inspirational people—from astronauts, policemen killed in 9/11, professors, and even Joe Paterno and his wife Sue. The artist ended up using an old picture—the one that was taken of me for the *Swimming World Magazine* High School Swimmer of the Year feature. The mural was completed a couple weeks later, and it looked wonderful. But it was weird seeing myself on the wall, smiling and so happy, recognized for all my accomplishments, when swimming made me feel like crying.

The trip to China was a great experience, despite my initial lack of interest in going. Corrie and I roomed together, and we met so many amazing athletes on the team. I also had the opportunity to see a totally different culture and explore the city of Beijing. I tried to make the best of each day. When I swam the 100-meter breaststroke, I tanked. I did not even come close to a personal best time or making it back to swim in the finals. I spoke to my parents that night on the phone, which helped me keep my head on straight. My father told me that no matter how I felt or how upset I was, I could pull off a great 50-meter. After talking to him about it, I started to believe him and gathered up a small amount of excitement about swimming the 50-meter breaststroke.

Sprinting always came fairly easy to me, and I enjoyed racing short events and decided that I did not want to leave the meet without accomplishing something (the way I left NCAAs a couple months prior). Feeling a little better about myself, I swam well and won a silver medal for my country. Coming in second was not a bad thing, because the winner was Tara Kirk, my USA teammate. I remember walking out with her and the bronze winner, waving to my USA team, and standing on the award podium. Our national anthem was played because an American won the gold, so it was a great experience and I felt good about being there. After coming back to the states, I had two weeks before practice started again—two weeks to step back and really think about what I wanted to do.

Chapter 8: Desperate for a Life Saver

After my trip to China, all I wanted was a break from swimming. And not just any break—I wanted to step away without a deadline so I wouldn't waste my whole break anticipating the day I had to swim again. I wanted to know that when I was ready to come back, I could come back. I talked to Bill and another coach, Ed, about my feelings on deck before practice, and we agreed that I could take the summer off from meets. I would still train with the team, but I didn't have to race. Because I was usually so unhappy at meets, about my times and not improving, this compromise sounded great to me. I could stay in shape, but not have to worry about the pressure of competing. And I realized that Bill and the other coaches were willing to work with me—they really were on my side.

My teammates, on the other hand, weren't as understanding. On any team, everyone has to take responsibility for their actions and do what everyone else on the team has to do. Allowing me to sit out of meets was definitely an exception the coaches made only for me, which was probably viewed as special treatment by all the other swimmers. Even my closest friends on the team didn't understand. Their body language let me know that they didn't want me around. We did the typical girl thing—ignore each other, rather than confront the issue—and we just drifted apart.

As the summer went on, I felt more and more alienated from the team. Instead of seeing my situation like the coaches were trying to help me, I started feeling like I was being singled out. I withdrew myself even more from the other swimmers and coaches. After classes started that fall, I was still not a fun person to be around. I was still not myself.

I looked for every excuse in the book to not train hard or go to team functions. Little things that I used to love were no longer important, such as leading the lane at practice, locker room jokes and gossip, and eating lunch with the team. Even the smell of chlorine when walking to the pool for practice made me sick to my stomach. My hands would start trembling when I attempted to put my cap and goggles on. My coaches and I constantly argued and the stress from practice and swimming consumed me. I got stomach aches at night when thinking about practice the next day. I had trouble sleeping and started taking shots of Nyquil to pass out. This was not healthy and definitely not normal behavior. Most athletes get nervous for a hard practice, but this feeling was beyond nerves—I had never felt like this before. It was intense anxiety, and all I wanted was to be happy again.

At a practice early in the fall, when we were still swimming outside, all my emotions and anxiety finally erupted in front of everyone on the team. Our assistant coach, John Retrum, had us practice a set of ten 100-yard freestyle (two laps in the long course pool) with a send-off time of 1:20, which meant every minute and twenty seconds, we should have been starting a new 100. But I was struggling and not making the send-off time. I knew I should have been making it with a few seconds of rest time to spare between each 100, but I lagged behind every time.

"Woodring," I heard John R. yell when I came up at the end of a lap. "If you don't break 1:20 on this next 100 then you're out of here!"

Oh god, I thought, as I pushed off the wall for my next 100. I had always struggled with freestyle, but I pulled myself as hard as I could through the water. I felt like I was trying. Still, I couldn't do it. Mentally, I wasn't there. As I swam, each stroke made me feel heavier and slower. And when I made it back to the wall, I hadn't made the send-off time. Everyone else swam past me in their lanes, already starting the next lap. John didn't say anything to me, but he didn't have to. I couldn't take it anymore. I was embarrassed, frustrated, and devastated all at the same time, and instead of following everyone on the next lap, I pulled myself out of the pool and threw a fit.

"This is bullshit," I yelled, loud enough for everyone in the pool to hear me. I ripped my goggles and cap off and threw them across the lawn. "I'm done. I'm out of here!"

I picked up my goggles and stomped through the grass in tears. The outdoor pool was located next to the indoor one, where the locker rooms were, and I walked up the little hill and pulled the natatorium door open. The pool was empty, and I sat down on a bench. The whole building was silent. I was so distraught and confused—I didn't know what just happened. I started thinking about John Pontz and how the situation might be different if he were here. And I thought about how embarrassed I was about swimming so poorly and what everyone else would think about me. Never, since I started swimming as a six-year-old, had I ever walked out of a practice—or had a coach threaten to throw me out. Everything felt like it was rushing past me at a million miles an hour, and I was so frustrated with myself.

"Just snap out of it," I said out loud to myself. "Go back out there and finish the set."

After sitting there a moment, I put my cap and goggles back on and slid into the indoor pool. I took a deep breath and then started swimming. The water helped me calm down, and I didn't think about swimming hard or accomplishing anything. I just swam the rest of the set on my own. I thought that if I went home and missed practice, I would hurt my training and therefore become even slower. I also thought that I could not bear to go back out there because of how I acted in front of John R. and the team. I did not want to be this person; I did not want my coach to throw me out of practice. And I didn't want to walk out. So although I probably looked like a crazy person, I swallowed my pride and went back outside to rejoin the team. We had about a half-hour to go, and John R. saw me get back in the water. But nobody said a word to me the rest of the workout. And I can only imagine what everyone was thinking. On the surface, the way I acted probably looked like I wanted attention. That's not how I felt at all. I didn't want anyone to talk to me, but I didn't want to leave and be alone in the locker room. I just wanted to finish.

When we were done practicing, John R. hung around and waited for me to get out of the pool. As he and I walked back to the natatorium, he said, "You know, that was the scariest thing I've ever had to do as a coach."

John was the youngest coach at PSU at that time—he was a graduate student, and had been a swimmer as an undergrad. When I was a freshman, he was a senior, so he knew the happy, normal Kristen. And John was a great coach. He was always there to help through hard workouts and find a way to put a smile on your face. When John had threatened to throw me out, I felt like he was picking on me. But then I realized that he was doing his job—pushing me to work harder. And he wouldn't baby me, like some of the other coaches might have. He told me he thought he'd get fired for throwing Kristen Woodring out of a practice, like Bill or one of the more senior coaches would have yelled at him. But he also knew something was wrong.

"What's going on with you?" he asked. "Usually when I challenge you, you rise to the occasion."

I apologized to him for the way I acted, but avoided his questions. I didn't feel like opening up, and I was a little afraid that if I did, everything would come out. I knew he was willing to talk, but I just couldn't, not right then. I was just happy that he was walking with me. Then I went back to the locker room and changed.

A couple days after that incident, John R. asked me to meet him at the HUB lawn on campus to talk about some things. I decided to go and see what he had to say—I was happy he wanted to meet with me, and I knew he wanted to talk about how I felt. I was comfortable talking to him because we had been teammates a few years before. He was very approachable and fun. The HUB lawn is a big grassy area on the Penn State campus where students are always hanging out. That afternoon it was crowded with kids on their way to class, people eating lunch, and girls sunning themselves on the lawn. It was a beautiful fall day and everyone around me looked so happy. I was miserable, though, and John could tell. We found a spot to sit on the grass and started talking about swimming.

Up until this point, not a single friend, family member, or coach had tried to talk with me or ask how I was feeling—even though I'd lashed out in front of the team and told my parents several times that I hated swimming. I told John about all the feelings I'd been having about swimming and my times and the pressure I felt to perform better than what I was doing. I told him I didn't mean to freak out at practice, but I had something in my head that wasn't going away. And instead of telling me to snap out of it and keep going, John was actually very caring and understanding.

John told me that he had a motto for himself: whenever you do something, do your best. And he said, "You know, if you don't feel like doing your best, or you can't do your best for whatever reason, then it's okay not to swim."

I had to think about what he said for a second before it sank in. It was okay not to swim? No one had ever told me that before. We sat on the lawn for over an hour, just talking and hanging out. And in that short time, I felt so much better. I had always been so concerned about what everyone else thought about me, but John helped me realize that swimming was just something I did, it wasn't who I was.

At the time I didn't fully understand. It took me a year to really be able to say this phrase and apply it. But that conversation planted a seed in my mind. It was a first step in looking at the sport of swimming in a different way. I was aware that swimming controlled my life, but I never really understood how much so until I got really depressed. When John and I finally sat down and talked, though, it was too late in my mind. I was so mentally gone and had taken myself out of that world that even when I tried to take his advice—to snap out of it and not take swimming to heart—I wasn't ready. I got what he was saying, and it did help me understand swimming in a different light, but I had already made up my mind that I needed to physically get away from the sport if I wanted to get better. I wasn't capable of training hard and changing my thoughts at the same time.

After that meeting with John, I kept thinking about what he said. It's okay not to swim. At first, the thought of not swimming was unbelievable to me. It was okay not to swim? But what about my team, what about my parents, what about my coaches? What would they all think? I knew most people didn't think very highly of me at that point because of the way I'd been acting the past couple months. But I also knew I was unhappy, and nothing seemed to be working. I thought a break from competing would help, but I didn't feel any better. Day in, day out, for almost a year, I had been unhappy. I was a full-scholarship athlete and had everything I could have wanted at my fingertips, and yet I couldn't remember the last time I was truly happy.

Over the next few days, when it came time to go to practice, I realized how much I didn't want to go get in the pool. It was as simple as that. I didn't want to get in the water. I didn't want to be in the locker room with the other girls. I just wanted to be away from it. And that's when I knew there was only one thing left for me to do: quit swimming.

Looking back, I realize I could have probably talked to my coaches about it and red-shirted for a year to keep my scholarship. But at the time, I didn't want to talk about it anymore. I didn't want to fight with my parents and coaches anymore—it wasn't getting me anywhere. No one took me seriously. Up until that point, quitting had only occurred to me in passing—a last resort type of thing. And I didn't really think about what my life would be like without swimming. I was just so desperate to change something. I just wanted to be happy.

It seems like such an easy thing to say or even, for some people, to do, but in my world, quitting swimming was very difficult. I would be letting many people down and not living up to the expectations they all had for me.

The following week, I wrote a letter to my head coach, listing the reasons why I wanted to end my swimming career. I had no goals or aspirations, I did not get nervous or feel adrenaline when racing, and I wanted to experience a normal life. I also knew that I wasn't a good influence for everyone else on the team—no matter how fast I was or how accomplished my career had been in the past, the team needed someone that could help keep morale up. Everything I had been thinking for over a year, I wrote in the letter. And I cried the whole time I wrote. I can even remember making a conscious effort not to let any tears drop on the paper.

I went to Bill's office the following day and, as I handed him my letter, my heart was pounding and my inner voice begged me to not cry. I was so worried he'd get mad at me. He read the letter and, to my surprise, responded with calm and understanding. He told me to take a week off and really think about my decision. He wanted to make sure I wasn't doing this on an impulse. But I told him I really didn't think more time would be necessary. My mind was made up. Some college athletes lose their passion for their sport, but when they are on scholarship and need the money to pay for school, they continue through the motions and find a way to keep going. But scholarship money or not, I couldn't find anything to keep me going.

"I knew this day would come," Bill said. "I knew you'd quit swimming, I just hoped it would be after you left Penn State." He explained that he remembered watching me swim at the 2000 Olympic trials and seeing my relationship with John and Kyle. We were inseparable, and he could see how unbalanced my life was prior to college and that one day I would burn out.

I was shocked by this, and confused. If my head coach had known for years that I would burn out, quit swimming, or be unhappy in college, why didn't he talk to me about it? Why did he watch me become miserable and so unstable for two years? But Bill had coached at the college level for a long time. He knew that with a handful of coaches and sixty or more swimmers on the team, no one swimmer ever got the attention John had given me before. Then I asked him why he hadn't talked to me when he saw me crying earlier that year at NCAAs, the last meet I swam. My teammate had seen him look at me and then keep walking—why didn't he say something? Bill said that he didn't want to say the wrong thing and make the situation worse. He had never been in that sort of situation before. He'd never coached someone who viewed swimming as her life, someone who allowed the sport to define her character.

It didn't matter anymore. I wrapped up the conversation and told him there was nothing he or anyone could say to make me change my mind. I needed to leave the team because I was not a positive person to be around. By continuing to act the way I was acting was not only destructive to me, but also harmful to my teammates. I used class as an excuse to leave and I walked out of his office. The minute I got outside, the tears came.

The fifteen-minute walk to my next class was very strange. I thought I would feel more relieved. I felt better knowing I did not have to practice that afternoon or the next day, but I still had the same sick feeling in my stomach. The next challenge was telling my parents, and I knew that would be more difficult than telling my head coach. I dreaded the conversation I had to have with my mom and dad.

I went to the rest of my classes that day, but did not take one note. My mind raced about how I was going to say the words, "I quit swimming today, Dad and Mom." Knowing that being on a full scholarship was a huge honor and accomplishment, the decision to quit swimming would be a major issue for my parents. In the months leading up to this point, they had heard me complain and say, "I hate swimming." But my dad's response was always about the program. He'd say, "You're a big girl now; if you don't want to swim at Penn State, you can transfer." But it wasn't about the program or going to another school. And for me, it wasn't about the scholarship.

Many athletes play a sport when they are young to try and earn a scholarship to college. Then some parents make their children play a sport so the child can earn a scholarship. I never swam for money. I never once thought about my full ride as a motivation to compete. Swimming and competing were things I loved and things that came effortless to me in the past. Being on a full scholarship at Penn State University came along with the territory. Being treated like one of the best was something that I grown accustom to. Getting priority scheduling for classes, free clothes, free jackets, free sneakers, free housing, and free food was just how my life went. But when I got in the water, it was because I wanted to do it.

Finally I got home that day and sat down to call my parents. Almost every conversation I'd had with my parents over the years had been about swimming—my times, how practice was going, my next meet, or whatever was coming up. We never really talked about anything else. When I called them that day, it was the same thing. I said right away, "I talked to Bill today, and I quit."

My father and mother, both on the other end of the line, were quiet for a long minute. Then my dad finally said, "Are you serious? Are you joking?"

I told them about my letter and how I just could not stand to swim for one more day. I told them I just wanted to be normal and experience college life without waking up at 5:30 a.m. every day and jumping in the pool. They were crushed. I could hear my mom crying. They did not understand how I could suddenly hate the one thing I had loved my whole life.

In disbelief, my dad asked, "Why would you want to be normal?"

At the time, I did not understand his question. All I wanted was a change because what I had been doing no longer made me happy.

My father said if I wanted to be a normal college student, he was going to show me what it was like. He emptied my bank account, which had been filled with scholarship money I had saved. He told me that because I gave up a full scholarship, I had to work my way through school, like a normal college student.

I was actually not too upset with his decision. I didn't expect anything less. I knew my father very well and could have predicted that this was the way he would handle the situation. My scholarship was very important to him, more important than it was to me. My dad had played baseball as a kid, but never excelled at it the way I excelled at swimming. And he and my mom had always been so proud and involved in my swimming career—they loved my lifestyle as much as I did, or as much as I used to love it, anyways. When I told them I quit, they felt like I was throwing all my talent away, and they were shocked. We got off the phone after just a few minutes.

With my father's challenge of paying for school on my own in mind, I quickly thought about jobs I wanted to apply for. I was actually excited about getting a job and working like other people. I had no job experience when it came to anything unrelated to swimming—while kids were working part-time jobs after school, I was always at practice. I had coached swim teams, counseled at swim camps, taught swim lessons, and life guarded—all the typical positions any swimmer had. Although I'd given up swimming competitively, I could still use my experience as a way to earn money. I applied at the local YMCA to be a swim instructor. Swimming lessons, I thought, would be a good weekend job, because the hours would be flexible. Knowing that I needed a couple options, I called the Penn State Natatorium and asked if I could coach the club team. The club team was called BCAT and it was made up of kids from age five to eighteen years old. But I also wanted to see what else was out there, and what else I would be good at.

As a hotel, restaurant, and institutional management major, I also decided to look for a serving position. I collected numerous applications at restaurants in downtown State College. I got accepted to work as a hostess, not a server, at The Deli Restaurant, downtown—I needed experience to wait tables. This was my parents' favorite restaurant—the one located directly across the street from the mural that I was painted on at the height of my swimming career freshman year.

Chapter 9: Retirement

I thought that if I quit swimming, everything in my life would improve. Like exhaling a sigh of relief, I envisioned my anxiety going away and being able to sleep better. I thought my grades would improve with so much extra time to study. And I thought I'd be happy again. But it wasn't that simple.

At first, I liked working at The Deli. I really wanted to learn the restaurant business, and I liked having a job and earning money—even though it was just a six-dollar-an-hour hosting job. Most of the people I worked with at the restaurant didn't know I was a swimmer, and I tried not to think about my past. Once I got to know some of my co-workers, I opened up a little.

"See that swimmer on the painting across the street?" I asked my boss, Sandra, one day.

"Yeah," she said.

"That's me."

"What?" She walked up closer to the window to get a better look.

"That's me. I used to be a swimmer." I told Sandra about how I had swum my whole life and about all my accomplishments from the past.

"If you were so good, why don't you go back?" she asked. "I'm sure they'd be happy to have you."

"Oh, no." I dismissed the idea immediately. "I'm retired."

After that day, Sandra asked me about swimming at big meets and practicing all the time. She used to play basketball, so she was interested in sports. But I always sugarcoated the story by leaving out the emotional details. I had entered a new phase in my life, I told her, and I was excited about it.

A girl from my high school, Liz, started working at The Deli around the same time I did. We were never very close in high school because I was always swimming and Liz had a normal social life. But at work, we had a good time together and we started hanging out all the time. After work on Tuesday nights, we'd go out together, which was something I'd never have dreamed of doing before. I always had practice early in the mornings, so going out on a week night was out of the question. The most I ever partied as a swimmer was having a few beers at a teammate's house on Saturday nights—under the watchful eye of the older swimmers. I never went to bars or frat parties before I quit swimming. All of that changed after I left the team—I had so much free time I could do whatever I wanted. I also reconnected with some of the girls from my team that ended up quitting before they graduated. My freshman roommate, Becky, had left the team the year prior. She and I also started hanging out again.

This free time started catching up to me, though. My grades didn't improve as I planned. With more free time, I put school aside and spent more time with my friends. The first semester without swimming was my lowest GPA ever. I enjoyed the freedom and being independent, but after a couple months it started to get old. On nights when business at The Deli was slow, I found myself staring out the window at my smiling face painted on the mural across the street.

The photo the artist used to paint me on the wall was the one that accompanied my *Swimming World Magazine* High School Swimmer of the Year profile. The day that picture was taken, I was training for Pan Ams with John and Kyle in Florida. My career had just started taking off and I was about to swim in my first international meet. Swimming was everything to me. And if someone would have told me then that four years later I'd give it all up, I never would have believed them.

Once the excitement of my new life started to wear off, my emotional state was right back where it was before I left the team—and maybe even worse. So many thoughts ran through my mind. I wanted to prove to myself, my parents, and everyone else that I could be happy without swimming and be successful at whatever I put my mind to. On the other hand, I knew that I had a god-given talent in swimming and I may not have fulfilled my career. I still cried uncontrollably and without reason. I just found myself in tears almost every day, and I still had trouble sleeping. Most nights I would lie in bed and stare at the ceiling. So I continued taking Nyquil to help me fall asleep.

At times I felt so panicked that I couldn't breathe. Nothing was going as I planned it. I was not any happier without swimming. Yes, I had more freedom and could go out with my friends. I learned how to work to pay for my own expenses, but it was not all it was cracked up to be. People think being a student-athlete is a great honor, and athletes are treated with such respect. I had always taken this for granted. And without realizing what I was doing, I kept wearing my Penn State swimming sweats to class so my classmates would still believe that I was an athlete.

One of my part-time jobs was coaching the Penn State age group team. This was difficult at first because they practiced in the same pool as the college team. My parents and friends didn't understand why I wanted to coach, especially because it was in the same building. I could run into someone from my team, and I had been so adamant about not getting back in the water when I quit. But I didn't have to get in the water to coach. I could stand on deck and do everything I needed to do. And being around the pool didn't bother me that much, as long as I wasn't swimming in it. One of the other coaches was a grad student named Rashanna. She had played tennis for Penn State as an undergrad, and she was working on her master's in sports psychology. She and I became good friends during that time—working together and traveling together with the team—and her interest in my swimming story helped me get a lot off my chest. The closer our friendship became, the more I told her about swimming. Whenever I needed someone to talk to about how I was feeling, she was always there for me.

After quitting swimming, my dad didn't call me for weeks. At first I was upset with him about this—I thought if he didn't want to call me, then I didn't want to call him either. When we did start talking again, it was hard to find things to talk about. My parents had been so involved in my swimming career that was the focus of all our conversations. Now they'd ask about school and work, but it all felt like small talk. When they came to visit and take me out to dinner on the weekends, I was quiet most of the time. And if I did talk to them, I would be negative and emotional. They knew I was struggling. My dad took me to the bookstore and bought me a few different self-help books, but none of them interested me. Something inside me felt like the answers I needed weren't going to be found in a book about thinking positive. I also made an appointment with a psychologist, at Bill's suggestion.

When I went to the appointment, I was already unsure about it because I didn't want to feel like a crazy person. When the psychologist started asking me the obvious questions like, "Are your parents divorced?" then I was sure it wasn't going to work. I didn't feel like starting from the very beginning and explaining my life to someone I didn't even know. I'm sure therapy works for some people, but I didn't have the energy to bring the therapist up to speed with my problems. Talking about all my problems was the last thing I wanted to do. I hardly said a word to the doctor during the appointment, and after that first time, I never went back. At the time, I believed I was burned out from swimming, and no stranger was going to make me happy or feel better about my situation. I didn't realize I was depressed and my feelings went beyond swimming. I thought it was all swimming related. I worried about who I was without the sport because I had never thought about life after swimming; I never prepared for when it was over. This uncertainty added to my depression and scared me a little bit. But being away from the sport, I started to see my problem was bigger than just swimming. It was how I defined myself as a person. I didn't realize that until I took swimming out of the equation and my feelings didn't change.

One Sunday night when I couldn't sleep and didn't want to call my dad, I called Rashanna in tears. She came over to my apartment just so I wouldn't be alone. She had noticed that Sunday nights were always the worst for me because it was the start of the new week. When I swam, on Sunday nights, I'd be mentally preparing for a week of tough practices. Without swim practice to occupy my mind, I was left to my thoughts and sadness. When Rashanna saw me crying and panicking like this, she never made recommendations about what she thought I should do. But she did help force me to think about what might make me happy by asking, "What do you want to do?"

Another night after going out with Becky, I slept at Becky's apartment so I wouldn't be alone. I had been fine all night when we were out, but when Becky and I were alone afterwards I started thinking about swimming and I started crying—which had become a pattern with me. Maybe Becky was fed up with me crying, and she said, "Kristen, if you want to swim, swim. If you don't, don't and just let it be that."

She wanted me to be okay with my decision. This was four months after I quit, and I was still struggling. I missed it, I missed being happy. "I don't know what I want to do," I told her. "I miss it, I miss being myself. I don't know what's wrong with me." I understood that Becky wanted to shake my sadness out of me, but I couldn't get a grip on why I felt so upset and why I couldn't get swimming out of my mind. It was a constant struggle. I quit swimming, but I thought about it all the time and I didn't feel satisfied. Changing my surroundings didn't work. I needed to change my way of thinking.

A few months before my sister's wedding, my mom, my sister, and I went on vacation to Florida. It was supposed to be a fun trip for all the Woodring girls before my sister got married and moved out, but I was so unhappy that I excluded myself from both of them and spend most of the time in the hotel room. I tried to lie by the pool, but could not stand the look or smell of the water. I felt ill, and couldn't bring myself to enjoy relaxing. One day when my mom and sister came back to the hotel from a shopping trip, they found me crying in bed and asked what was wrong. I had no answer. I couldn't express why I felt sad; I just did.

Then in February, something happened that changed my life forever. It was a normal Friday night and a few of my girlfriends and I were planning on going to a frat party. Everyone met at my house to hang out beforehand, and we bought some beer to drink, just like we did every weekend. By the time we left for the party, I had been drinking for a few hours. I volunteered to drive because I had the biggest car and there were about five girls in our group. I felt okay to drive and we weren't going far. After the party, we went downtown to get pizza at a place that stayed opened late. Everything was fine until we all got back in my car to go home. The entrance to the parking lot was located off a one-way alley that connected in less than a car's length to College Avenue, the main road. Instead of going left and taking the one-way street all the way down and backtracking to the main road, everyone always ignored the one-way on the alley and took a right to get back on the main road. It was one of those things that everyone always did, and that night I did it too. But at night, I guess police officers sit there and wait for people to ignore the one-way sign so they can pull them over.

On my way out of the parking lot, I spotted a police car pull up behind me. I immediately panicked. At the time, I was only twenty—just a few months away from the legal drinking age. I wasn't swerving or acting wild and drunk, but State College was pretty aggressive about catching drunk drivers. And at that time of night, the cop had to know I'd been out. I was nervous and drove with extreme caution, with all my friends laughing and having fun, almost oblivious, in the back seat. The cop followed me a couple blocks down College Avenue and finally put his lights on.

I pulled over and got my license and registration ready for the officer. I knew I might get a ticket, but I didn't think I'd get in trouble for drinking—I thought I was fine. However, looking back, when he came to my window, he had to have smelled alcohol. All five of us in the car had been drinking beer all night. And sure enough, he asked me to step out of the car. Right on the busy street, he had me do a roadside test to see if I was drinking. He had me walk in a straight line and he had me balance on one foot and touch my nose. The whole time I thought I was doing fine. I was scared, but I wasn't terrified because I really thought he'd let me go. I had never been in trouble for anything. But then he gave me a breath-alyzer. I think I blew a .08, but because I was underage, anything was illegal. So I failed and I was arrested for a DUI. He put me in the police car and asked one of my friends to drive my car home. It was the scariest moment in my life. All I could think about was what my parents were going to think.

The police officer didn't take me to jail; he actually took me to the campus hospital and had them draw my blood for an alcohol test. I went through all the procedures and soon after that they told me I was free to go.

Liz picked me up and took me home, but I did not get a wink of sleep that night. I couldn't stop thinking about the direction my life was going. I felt as though my parents were already disappointed with me about quitting swimming and losing my scholarship, and now a DUI. This was not who I was. This was not how I envisioned my life.

I called my parents early the next morning to tell them what happened. When my dad picked up the phone I told them I got in trouble the night before, and he guessed right away that I got a DUI. He said he had a feeling something like that would happen because he knew I drank with my friends and he saw unhealthy patterns in my behavior. He always asked me to take the bus when I went out with my friends, but we thought of the bus as such an inconvenience. Surprisingly my parents were not too upset about the DUI, though. I think they were relieved I wasn't hurt.

Getting a DUI was a horrible thing in my life, not only because I lost my license for a year and had to pay a hefty fine, but also because it was so unlike me. Something had to give. I was not acting like myself, and I didn't want people around me to think I had turned into a person who got in trouble. This was not the person that I wanted to be. I thought about what I had to do to turn my life around. I thought back to before I came to college and what had made me such a happy person. All the memories that came to my mind included swimming.

Chapter 10: The Comeback

When I quit swimming, I avoided the water. Even when I was coaching I spent most of my time on deck. But there was this one boy—probably thirteen or fourteen years old—who always tried to get me to swim. He knew I used to swim for Penn State and that I had set records, but he didn't know the circumstances around why I quit. Because he was at that cocky, pre-teen age, he wanted to see if he could beat me in a race. Every practice, he'd bring it up. But I always brushed him off, saying, "No, no, I don't swim anymore." Not only was I hesitant to get in the water, but I would be embarrassed if he beat me.

For months, this same boy asked me to race him. Then finally, when we were away for a meet, I gave in. "All right, all right. Let's do it," I said.

Rashanna was there and she knew it had been about six months since I'd gotten in the water. She was so excited to watch me swim. So right after the meet, when everyone was heading to the locker room to get changed and get ready to leave, he and I got in the water. I wasn't in for long—we raced to the end of the pool and back. I beat him too; he was just a kid. But when I got out of the water I remember thinking, "That wasn't that bad." It was actually kind of fun.

Having fun in the pool that day wasn't enough to make me go back to swimming, but it was a step in the right direction. Seeing him and his excitement and innocence was refreshing and made me remember how fun swimming used to be for me. It was also cool I had this talent where I could just jump in the water and beat him.

I grew up Catholic, and when my parents came to visit me on weekends, I always went to church with my mom. Without swimming, I found church kind of comforting and started going whether my mom was in town or not. I always went through the motions of church, but I never forced myself to be spiritual and never applied faith to my life and the way I thought. Once I started connecting my faith to my life, I realized I had been making poor choices about the people I surrounded myself with and the decisions I made. Drinking and driving was the primary example—these were unhealthy behaviors and I could have really gotten hurt. My DUI could have been a lot worse, but it wasn't, and so I felt like someone was watching over me. I knew it was supposed to teach me something. Instead of being bitter and losing my faith, I realized everything happens for a reason and started thinking about how my experiences could make me a better person. Instead of being ashamed of my DUI, I wanted to learn from it and make sure it never happened again.

I started trying to change the way I looked at life and being thankful for my health and everything I did have. Rather than look at the fact that I didn't win a race and I didn't go to Stanford, I was healthy, I was at a good school, and I had a supportive family who was always there. Thinking about this on a daily basis helped me change. Church gave me time to think about how blessed my life really had been. There were times when I was so unhappy, when I wished I was the NCAA champion and when I was bitter that I didn't get to go to Stanford. But I had accomplished so many things, including a full scholarship just because I was so good at swimming. When I took a step back and looked at my whole life, I had always been so lucky and never realized it before. Now I was wasting the talent God had given me.

Since faith began playing a role in my everyday life, my anxiety started going away. I was able to sleep and I continued to think about swimming in a positive way. I didn't really miss the physical part of practicing and competing, but I did miss being part of the team. I missed hanging out with everyone and being part of a group of people who were so similar to me. I wanted to be happy again, and I couldn't escape the feeling that, to be happy, I had to swim again.

When Big Tens came around in February, I was glued to my computer watching the live results of the meet. When I quit, I never imagined caring what the team was doing without me. But I ended up crying most of the weekend because I knew I could have been there to help the team. I wasn't worried about winning or setting records; I realized that without doing those things, even if I swam my worst, I could still score points. Seeing all my former teammates' scores pop up on my computer screen made me miss being there with them. I missed riding the bus, I missed going to dinner after meets, and I even missed wearing the same team outfit as everyone else.

Not long after Big Tens, I realized I wanted to go back. I wanted to be part of the team. I wanted to finish what I'd come to Penn State to do. I wanted to swim again.

I was a talented swimmer—God made me this way. I had to do what I was put on this earth to do. I knew I had to go back, but I had to do it the right way. I didn't want anyone to think I was crazy or just trying to get attention. I was a different person. Now I knew swimming didn't define me and no matter how I swam, I should be having fun. I was ready.

The first step was telling my parents. I didn't want to do it over the phone, so I asked them to come to State College for the weekend. My mom had a commitment and couldn't make it, but my dad came, thinking this was just like any other visit. When we went to dinner, I told him I had something I wanted to talk to him about. I warned him that it wasn't anything bad, but he might be surprised. He looked a little nervous—after quitting swimming, getting a DUI, and everything else that had happened, he was just waiting for the next crisis I could drop on him.

Then I finally said, "I have been thinking about swimming again."

My dad smiled from ear to ear. "This is great! We have to tell Bill right away," he said. "We need to get moving."

"Calm down, Dad," I said. "If I do this, things have to be different." I explained to my dad that I wanted him to be there to support me, but I didn't want him to be as involved as he had been before. My dad is a very passionate person and I love him, but I couldn't take the pressure of swimming to please my parents. I wanted him to support me, whether I swam good or bad, and not say a word either way.

"Okay, okay," he said, still smiling. "Whatever you want."

When I told my parents I was thinking about swimming, I was about 90 percent sure I wanted to do it. One concern was that I'd just want to quit again. But also, if I went back after a year off, I wouldn't be able to swim at the level I used to compete at. There was no way I'd be good. At first, I wasn't sure I'd be okay with that. Would I be able to overlook my times and still have fun swimming? Plus, because of the way I'd quit, I wasn't sure my teammates would welcome me back. Anticipating their reaction made me the most nervous.

After thinking about it for a few more days, I e-mailed Bill to set up an appointment with him. Going into the meeting, I wasn't completely sure how he'd react. When I swam for him, he wasn't exactly down to earth. He could be difficult to approach because he was always so serious, and I was afraid he wouldn't understand. But when I walked into his office that day, he surprised me.

"Hey Kris, how are you doing?" he asked me. He smiled, and I immediately felt a little less nervous.

"I've been good," I said. "I wanted to talk to you because I've been thinking about swimming again and I think I'm ready to come back." Before he could answer, I made sure he knew the reason why. "I want to finish what I started," I said. "I don't want my scholarship money back, and I don't want you to think that's the reason I'm here. And I don't want to be the center of attention—I just want to be one of the team."

Initially, his feelings were mixed. He asked me to think about it for a month and make sure I was coming back for the right reasons. I told him I had no intentions of causing conflict and I knew I probably wasn't going to be as fast as I was in the past. I was ready to be happy with just being a member of the squad. I told him I missed the little things about the sport, such as the bus rides, locker room chat, and friendships with the girls and coaches—all the things I'd taken for granted all my life.

"I still want you to take some time to think about it," he repeated. "But the door is always open."

"Do you think I should meet with the team to let them know?" I asked.

"Actions speak louder than words, Kris, and if you come to practice, work hard, and maintain a positive attitude, then that will be enough."

When I left Bill's office that day, I felt good. But I wanted to make sure that when I came back to swimming, I made right by my teammates. I did not just want to show up on the pool deck one day and surprise everyone. So I called the captain of the swim team and asked her if I could meet her for lunch to talk about some things.

The captain was a year younger than me. She was an excellent student and an okay swimmer. But she was dedicated and a positive role model. So Bill appointed her captain her sophomore year instead of choosing a senior, which was always the tradition. However, as soon as she heard my voice on the other end of the phone, she made it clear that I wasn't welcome on her team.

"What could you possibly have to say, Kristen?" she said.

"I just need to talk to you about something."

"Fine. Meet me at Panera Bread Company at 12:00 sharp."

Her mood hadn't softened when we met the next day. Sensing her impatience, I cut right to the chase. I told her I was going to come back to swimming and re-join the team. I will never forget her reaction: "You are the most selfish person I've ever met. If it were up to me, you'd never swim for Penn State again."

I was crushed, but I knew she wasn't going to welcome me back with open arms. She'd seen the way I behaved before I left, and she probably thought I just wanted to get back in the spotlight. She was protecting her team, and I understood that.

I repeatedly told her, as tears streamed down my face, I was not coming back to be a superstar or try to break records. I simply wanted to help the team and complete my career. I knew the way I acted before I quit was unacceptable and during my time away from swimming I learned many things. I truly loved the sport and I wanted to finish what I started. I wanted to help the program become better and help the team be the best it could be.

She then went on to tell me that it was not her decision, and if I was going to swim again, she could not do anything about it. Before leaving, she told me, "We don't have to be friends; we just have to be teammates."

Quitting swimming was one of the hardest things I've ever done, but coming back was going to be even harder. The captain was mad, and she had some right to be. But she had no idea what I felt and she didn't understand anything I had been through. Her reaction hurt me and I felt so misunderstood. But I'd said what I needed to say, and I decided to leave it at that. I couldn't control her thoughts and feelings, all I could do was lead my life the best way I could and treat others the way I wanted to be treated. I decided to let my actions and hard work speak for itself.

Before team practice started, I wanted to get in the water a few times on my own. Since I left the team, the only time I swam was when I raced that boy on the team I coached. Starting when I was six years old, the longest I'd ever been out of the water was two weeks. If I wanted to make it through the first practice, I needed to get back in shape and get used to being in the water swimming for so long. So I decided to go to the pool a few times to see what it would be like to put my suit, cap, and goggles on and swim. At first, getting in the water was a little intimidating. I stood at the edge of the pool and listened to the clear water gently slap the sides. It was like the final decision that had to be made. And saying I was going back was a lot easier than physically getting in the water. But I had to get it over with—I just had to get in and go. I couldn't let swimming be bigger than me. Even those little workouts had to be just exercise, just something I did. I couldn't let myself get all worked up about it; I had to learn how to get in the pool, swim, and then leave it at that. So I dove in and swam.

Team practice started in April. My main goal was to prove I belonged on the team and finish swimming with my original class. My class started freshman year with eleven boys and six girls, and when I went back, it was down to two boys and three girls. For whatever reason, they all quit the team. Finishing all four years as a student-athlete was an accomplishment in itself.

I worried in those first days back about little things, like where I was going to sit and who I was going to partner up with for exercises. Part of the team was very understanding and accepted me back. Sally, the same girl who saw Bill walk past me when I was crying at NCAAs, talked to me and we slowly rebuilt our friendship. She hadn't called me at all after I quit, and she never apologized for it or asked how I was doing, but I didn't hold a grudge for that. Bill mentioned it to me one day. After practice he pulled me aside and said, "I see you buddying up to Sally, and that's fine and good. But why didn't she call you when you quit or try to reach out to you then?" To me, it wasn't a big deal. She may not have known what to say to me then. But she was my friend before and I was happy to have her as a friend again.

There were, however, and couple girls who resented me for my decision to quit and were not too thrilled to see my back at practice. Most of the girls on the team were younger, so if they knew me at all, they probably only remembered the negative, miserable me. My friendship with Courtney, who I had been so close with before, changed. She had made new friends and we grew apart. I decided I was not going to hate those girls; I was going to show them I was serious about being a better person and swimmer.

I worked my butt off day in and day out and struggled to finish every practice. Especially during the first weeks, I wasn't in good enough condition to finish practice strong. By the end my arms were numb. The dry-land workouts were easier than swimming, so I decided to come to practice early to do an extra thirty minutes of cardio to try and speed up getting back into shape. Completing a two-hour practice in the water was grueling. Coach was nice enough to give me my own lane when he saw I was falling behind. He did this mainly to get me out of the way, but also to let me finish at my own pace. And I was happy Bill was so willing to give me time and work with me.

In the beginning my emotions were a daily struggle. I made a conscious effort to make the choice to be happy and control myself. As each day passed, I felt happier and more like my life was going in the right direction. I had to wake up and choose to be happy and content with my life and thankful I was a good swimmer and able to help the team. Most of the girls eventually softened up and started accepting me. For me, that was the best thing—being part of the team again. I let myself enjoy the fact that I was an athlete again and able to experience the honor of being part of a collegiate sport. Even the little things were great, like getting our suits and gear, and practicing so hard and then heading into the locker room exhausted together. I loved the team atmosphere.

During the first couple of dual meets, I did not swim like the old Kristen. I would come in third or fourth and my times were nowhere near where they used to be. At first, this made me cringe and feel upset, but I was determined to not let my times predict my emotions. I made a conscious effort not to get mad at myself or frustrated. As long as I trained hard, had fun, and did the best I could, I was going to be happy with anything. It sounds silly, but I really had to learn how to lose. Bill also put me on the B relay team, which, looking back was a good thing. Bill made me earn my spot on the A team—he didn't do me any favors. And this made me better appreciate where I had been when I quit.

By Christmas, though, I was back in shape. I started swimming better, and I even earned my scholarship back for spring semester. Bill said he was proud of me and I proved to him that I was serious about the sport. My times continued to improve through the beginning of the season and I quickly was at the top of the Big Ten conference again in the 100-yard breaststroke. I qualified for NCAAs and I earned my spot on the A relays. But I tried not to get too wrapped up in it—knowing that if I didn't swim well, I wouldn't be too disappointed. Most of all, I really enjoyed spending time with the girls on the team. Practice no longer scared me, and I didn't think too much about not swimming a personal best time. Competing was enough for me. I also didn't worry about staying up a little late or going to dinner with friends on a night before practice. I knew it wouldn't kill me, and because of this I enjoyed my life at college so much more than I had before.

Leading into Big Ten Championships, I felt a great drive to win. I did not worry about what my time was going to be, but I wanted to win back the title. I also really wanted the team to win. My sophomore year they had won—it was the first time the Penn State women won a championship. But I was so upset about my time that I was crying and didn't really enjoy the experience of being on the Big Ten champion team. I wanted that chance again.

I swam great at the championship meet, and going into my events I had no fears or anxieties about making a best time. My 200 medley relay team won, and I won my third Big Ten title in the 100-yard breaststroke. I did it! And my time actually improved a little since the last time I was there. When I won my freshman year, I swam a 59.7 and my sophomore year my time increased to 1:01. This year I swam a 1:00.37.

The team swam incredibly well and for a while we were on track to win our second Big Ten team championship. In swimming, the divers contribute to the team's total point score. And Penn State had good divers, but the school didn't have platforms at the pool, which meant we didn't have anyone competing in the platform dive event—the last event of the weekend. So while all the other teams competed and earned points, we couldn't gain any because we didn't have anyone to compete. I remember standing with my teammate, Sally, watching the other teams earn points with tears streaming down my face. Not seeing any PSU divers, I knew we didn't have a far enough lead to keep it without anyone in that event. Here I was, crying at Big Tens, again. This time, though, I wasn't crying because I didn't win or didn't go a best time; I was crying because I wanted the team to win so badly. In the end we got second by only a couple points and I can remember our hearts ached not winning the team title. Coming that close and only losing the meet by a couple points was an awful feeling. I put every ounce of energy I had into helping out—we just came up a little short. We all lost together. And this time around I really appreciated being one of the team.

Even though we did not win, I was thrilled with how the meet went and had so much fun with my teammates. My intense competitive nature wasn't completely gone, but definitely was not what it used to be. Actually, going into races, felt more relaxed and centered—able to live in the moment while swimming my hardest.

The NCAA Championships were pretty similar to Big Tens. I had great individual swims and our relays also swam well. I placed seventh in the 100 breaststroke, which qualified me to be an automatic All-American. The emotions I felt this time around were very different from my last trip to NCAAs. Before I'd been crying after every race—I was such a mess that my dad yelled at me in front of a huge crowd. This time I did not feel extremely high or extremely low. My emotions were very level, no matter how great or how bad I swam. I enjoyed the preparation and experience of being there with the team a lot more than what the clock read.

I made the 2004 Olympic Trial cut that year, too, and decided to train through the summer with Penn State to swim at trials in California. I knew I wasn't going to rank as high as I had four years prior, but I still wanted to compete at the meet. The summer went very well and I loved being at Penn State with my teammates. At trials, I was thrilled to race, but it was a different experience because I wasn't one of the top breaststrokers competing that year. I had no thoughts that I'd win. It was more exciting watching the meet and all the amazing swimmers make the Olympic Team, than it was for me to actually swim. My time was a 1:12.92 and I placed twenty-ninth. I didn't make the top sixteen, but I realized that coming back to the sport after a year off and swimming fast enough to qualify for the Olympic trials was a feat in itself. At that point, I had no regrets. I thought the 2004 Olympic trials would be the perfect ending to my career.

I did run into John Pontz at trials. Kyle wasn't there—he had finished his senior year at Georgia and decided to retire. But John was there with his team. Every time I saw John I was excited to see him, and I gave him a big hug. We were like old high school buddies. But it was a little weird at the same time because he wasn't my coach anymore.

At the end of each swim season, most teams have a banquet to hand out coach's gifts and awards for swimmers. The banquet my senior year was a great moment to be a part of, and at the time I thought that would be my last team event. By then I had realized what a wonderful decision it was for me to come back to the team. I wanted to help the team succeed, get back on track with making smart decisions, surround myself with positive people, and finish what I came to college to accomplish. I wanted to know I ended my swimming career on a good note, rather than leaving the team with such hate and anger. I definitely was happy with how I swam and how many great memories I gained by deciding to swim my senior year.

I had come back a different swimmer. I had been on a destructive path my sophomore year—I was hurting my team, my relationships with my family and friends, and myself by not knowing how to leave my emotions out of the sport. I had wrapped my whole life up so tight in swimming that I was drowning. If I hadn't taken that year off to clear my head, I don't know what would have happened to me. Looking back, taking that year off was one of the best decisions I ever made. I was a better person and a better athlete because of it.

After the banquet was over, my assistant coach came up to congratulate me. When we hugged, he whispered, "It would be great to have you swim one more year. You have the eligibility and we need a breaststroker."

This caught me off guard. Could I really come back? Did I really want to? The fact that I took a year off gave me another year of eligibility to swim. I knew this, but I had no intentions to do so. When I made my decision to come back to the team, I wanted to finish with my class and retire. The thought of swimming one more year, with a senior class that was not my own, did not seem too appealing. But at the same time, I had another year left of school. So I did not write off the decision just yet. I smiled and told my coach I would think about it and let him know.

Chapter 11: One More Year

Right after NCAAs, the year I had thought would be my last year swimming, I got a note from Megan, the teammate I roomed with at the championship meet. She was a freshman that year, and I've kept her note all these years. It read:

Kristen,

I would just like to take this opportunity to thank you for making my first year at Penn State a memorable one. I feel very privileged to swim in the same pool and share the same goals with a woman of great character who owns a heart pure of gratitude.

While the first couple months here at school were challenging and difficult to handle, the entire team made me feel welcomed and loved. There were times when I wanted to quit and give up on all my goals and hard work. After spending an amazing week with you in Texas at NCAAs, I finally felt like I met the real Kristen. By hearing your struggles and times of disappointment in the beginning of the year, I realized we were both in the same boat. But you overcame your fears of rejection with the team and are swimming as fast as you did before you took a break. Now every day when I struggle with life, I am able to use you as a motivation to stick it out and get back on top.

I remember the word you chose at the Florida training trip to put on your key chain: GUTS! When you spoke about getting up and racing with heart every time, no matter how you felt, my swimming changed for the better. You helped me to realize my biggest weakness: I focus too much on how I feel in the water instead of focusing on my strengths and hard work that would carry me to success. While you may not have realized the impact you've had on me, I truly believe that a large part of why I had such a good season is because of you.

I have truly enjoyed these past weeks we have gotten to know each other. You are an amazing swimmer, teammate, and person—a true team player. I hope that you will be joining us next year for one more season, one more year of success, and hopefully a year where you can lead our team to unity. You are one of my biggest inspirations and I will always look up to you.

I am truly blessed to have met you and thank you for your words of wisdom and motivation!

Love always,

Megan

Megan's note, plus the urging of my coaches, made the decision to swim my fifth year at Penn State an easy one to make. And after my senior banquet, I only thought about it for a few more days before I decided to go ahead and do it. With another year of classes, I would be on campus anyway, so I might as well help the team. My fifth year would be like a bonus year and another chance to go after the Big Ten team title. The fact that we came so close my senior year and did not win it was heart wrenching. We would only lose two seniors if I came back and we were gaining a great freshman class. We definitely had the talent to win, and this would be a great way to finish my swimming career. It would also show the team and coaches that I truly cared about Penn State swimming.

By the time I started training for my last year, I had such a clear head. My anxiety was gone because I chose to swim—no one pressured me in any way. I was, however, like the old lady on the team—I didn't have a class because everyone else graduated, so I was grouped in with the year below me. And the swimmers in the freshman class coming in were five years younger than I was. They all had heard that I'd quit and come back to the team, but it was nice that they didn't know me before my break. They didn't have anything to hold against me, like some of the senior girls.

I continued to train hard and enjoy the last moments I had as a Penn State athlete. The women's team was focused throughout the year and determined to make an impression at the Big Ten Championships come February. Having a second-place finish the previous year was a great motivator and the whole team trained with such a singleness of purpose—we wanted to win at Big Tens. The team got together without the coaches for meetings to stay motivated and on the right track, and we wrote our goals on a chalkboard where they were always visible. We felt that we had a great chance of regaining the title, which Penn State had won for the first time my sophomore year.

I tried to make the best of each dual meet, practice, and team activity. My feelings about this being my last year were mixed. I was excited, but sometimes when the senior class would count down the days and practices we had left we would cry because we knew we would never be a part of something as special as Penn State swimming again. At the same time, I realized how far I'd come over the years. I saw all the freshmen girls struggle with adjusting to college life and our intense practice regimen. Transitioning from high school to college is difficult for everyone, but it can be particularly difficult for athletes. I found a study, "Comparing Sources of Stress in College Student Athletes and Non-Athletes" by Gregory Wilson, P.E.D. University of Evansville, and Mary Pritchard, Ph.D. Boise State University, that suggested athletes have a harder time adjusting because they have more extensive demands on their time, they can get injured, they often lose the star status that came with being high school athletes, and they have to worry about the possibility of being benched or cut from their team. The article also said that most freshmen student-athletes are unprepared to successfully deal with these stressors. And I could see how the freshman girls got so down on themselves if they didn't swim well or if they had trouble with a workout. All of their challenges were familiar to me, and I remember sitting down with a few different girls and offering some encouragement. I told them that even though they didn't always feel like it, they were doing fine and just to do their best and keep going.

During a workout in the weight room, one of the coaches got in one of the freshman girls' face and yelled at her about working harder. The coach was just picking on her a little to toughen her up—I knew this because he did the same thing to me when I was a freshman. But she got so upset about it and started crying. Later I went to her dorm to talk to her and try to make her feel better. I told her what happened in the weight room that day was something we'd all been through and not to take it personally. The coach was just pushing her—he didn't hate her or think she was a bad swimmer. He was treating her the same way he treated everyone else.

"I'm not going to sit here and tell you it's going to be easy," I said. "But look at how lucky we are—we get free clothes and free sneakers. We're different from most other students at Penn State. But you're going to have days like this." I think I helped her a little; I know I wished I had an upper classmen to help me gain a healthier perspective in those early years.

We had a great dual meet season and I was swimming fairly well. I tried to not get caught up in my times and still appreciate the experience of each meet and the joy of being on relays. During the Christmas training trip in Naples, Florida, I had a great two weeks of practice. Each day it seemed as though I was training faster and getting closer to the level I had been at when I was a freshman. As I improved, my expectations for the end of the year started to change and I began focusing on one thing . . . being the first woman to win the 100-yard breaststroke at Big Tens four times. It was a very reasonable goal, I thought, and I knew if I stayed on track and continued to put 100 percent into practice, I would have a great shot at accomplishing my goal.

Breaking a minute and getting a personal best time also crossed my mind, but I knew if I focused on a certain time I might forget about the process by which to achieve it. I also knew that even if I trained hard, ate well, and stretched, I would never reach the level I had been at when I trained with John for the 2000 Olympic trials. Penn State was a completely different situation—I was one out of thirty girls who needed attention. And my stroke technique was not as sharp as it used to be. To break a minute in the 100 breaststroke was far out of my reach, I thought. But I did want to make my mark on the Big Ten division, if nothing else.

In the final days before Big Tens, I knew I had to swim a smart race if I wanted to win. I had always been a natural sprinter and when I raced I always swam as hard as I could for as long as I could, which often meant I'd exhaust myself towards the end of the race. My teammate, Courtney, who was seated first going into the meet was much better at pacing herself. She always knew how to save extra energy for the final lap. She was great at building into the 100. For this reason, she was also an awesome 200 swimmer. Knowing I could not swim the 100 like I used to and sprint each lap, I had to be smart and pace myself for the back half of the race.

During the morning preliminary swim, I watched Courtney swim an amazing 100 breaststroke and clock in at 1:01.60. This was a great time, and I knew I had my work cut out for me. I was in the next heat and swam as fast as I could for all four laps. As I made my turns, I saw that I was far ahead of my heat. When I touched the wall and looked up to see my time, it read 1:01.90. I was a little disappointed because I was going into finals still seated second. But I tried not to worry about it too much. I just needed to focus and get ready for the final race. The team as a whole was swimming so well. We were leading the meet from the beginning and kept increasing our point total and moving further head with each event.

Because my teammate had a faster time that day, I assumed she'd be on the A relay team for finals that night as well. This was okay with me. I had been on the relay every year, so she could have it this year. A few years ago I probably wouldn't have seen it that way, but it was okay. She beat me fair and square. So I went back to the hotel with the team, had lunch, and took a nap. I also watched my race from the morning swim to see if I could give myself an edge that night. Seeing myself swimming, I definitely knew I needed to slow it down in the first half and really turn up the speed during the last two laps. I was lucky I still swam a decent time and got to swim in a middle lane. But my teammate's time was really good and she would be tough to beat.

At around four that afternoon we all met to head back to the pool for finals that evening. Then on the bus ride, Bill stood up and talked to the team for a few minutes about the meet.

"All you have to do is go out there and do your job tonight," he said. "We have a strong lead, and to keep it you don't have to do anything extraordinary. Just do your job."

My nerves set in during the bus ride. I tried to listen to music and relax, but knew this was going to be my last 100 breaststroke ever in the Big Ten. As I thought more about it, excitement and adrenaline rushed throughout my body. I knew I was going to accomplish something great. Not one negative thought entered my mind, and I felt that winning was in my reach.

Then while we were all warming up at the pool, Bill pulled me aside and surprised me.

"I am putting you on the Medley relay tonight," he said.

"Oh my god," I said, knowing this decision went against the norm. "Are you sure?"

"I know your experience, and I'm going with you," he said. I could tell he'd been thinking about it all day, and he didn't want to do anything to risk losing the championship. Of course I wasn't going to let him down, so I said okay.

The relay was my first swim that night, and all four of us on the Penn State team swam so well that we won. This was a great start for the team and we lengthened our lead. I had a great spilt, which also helped my confidence going into the 100 breast. When it came time to go to the ready room with the other seven finalists, I was very relaxed and focused. I took in each moment and wanted to appreciate walking out, waving to the crowd of parents and teammates, and swimming my last 100 breaststroke at the Big Ten Championships. So many thoughts ran through my mind. I thought back to the difficult and emotional road that got me to this point. When I quit swimming I never thought I'd be back in this place—now this was the only place I wanted to be. I had no regrets and was so thankful to be in this moment. I could not have had a better experience during the past two years back in the swimming world, and I had one more thing to do . . . win!

The announcer went through the lanes and announced each girl and a few of her accomplishments. When he got to my lane, he stated I was the current Big Ten record holder and reigning champion. Then he said something I will never forget: "For the last time . . . Kristen Woodring!" The last time—this choked me up a little, but definitely put a huge smile on my face. I could not have been more ready than I was at that moment.

As the gun went off and I dove in, I controlled my excitement and paced the first two laps. I was slightly behind the girl who was in the lane next to me. My parents in the stands were panicked. Throughout my whole career, I had rarely, if ever, came back to win a race. If I were going to win, I was usually ahead the whole time. But as I made my second turn with 2 laps to go, I came up and started to pick up the pace. I felt myself getting faster and pulling ahead. My last turn, I was in the lead by a small margin. So I put it all on the line. I had to dig deeper than I'd ever dug before. I pushed myself and swam with such determination, just trying to get to the wall as fast as I could. When I touched and turned to look at the scoreboard, there was a number one next to my lane! My time was 1:01.41 and my teammate, who took second with a 1:01.55.

I got out of the water and headed back to my team. I didn't want to celebrate too much because knowing Courtney got second—I wanted to be a good sportsman instead of rubbing it in her face. The fact that Penn State had girls place first and second was a special thing. I kept my cool, hugged and smiled at everyone, and made my way to the warm-down pool. My heart was pounding and I was dripping wet. As I started putting my goggles back on, I felt someone come up and grab me from behind. It was my dad, giving me a bear hug. At first, I was surprised—he wasn't allowed down on the deck. "Dad," I said, "what the heck are you doing down here?"

For him it was an emotional race. He had been anticipating the moment when I won another title—weeks before the race, he had a license plate made that said "PSU 444"—and now that I had done it, he was overcome with emotion. He hugged me, kissed me on the cheek, and said, "Great job, baby."

"Thanks, Dad," I said. "Now get back up there."

I was truly blessed and could not have asked for a better finish to my career. Three years prior I had also won by the skin of my teeth and instead of being happy, I was miserable. Now, in the same meet, same event, and pretty much the same turnout, I could not have been happier. I finally learned to appreciate the feeling of doing my best, being thankful for talent, and enjoying the moment.

Penn State went on to win the meet by a record-setting margin. Our final team total score was 693, a school record. The second place team, Indiana, had scored 497. At the end of the meet, when we were getting our t-shirts, hats, and trophy, I appreciated every second. The whole team, including the coaches, jumped in the water to celebrate. We stayed at the pool as late as we could and basked in our glory. While floating in the water with my warm-ups on, I looked around at what was happening and realized how lucky I was to have a second chance to enjoy being a part of the champion team.

Chapter 12: Ending on a High Note

That night after Big Tens, when we were all back at our hotel rooms, Bill called me and asked me if we could talk. I met him outside his room a few minutes later and I could tell something was bothering him. We sat down in the hallway and he asked me, "Do you think I did the right thing tonight?"

"Bill, you made the decision and put me on the relay because you knew I knew what I was doing," I told him.

"I understand what you have to go through with the girls," he said. "But I have seen you grow up so much, and you really accomplished a great thing tonight."

We sat there and talked for a while, and had such a great conversation. This was the first time Bill and I had really talked like friends. And I was glad after all these years of working together, we finally understood each other.

After winning Big Tens, the only meet left was NCAAs a few weeks later. Eight or nine Penn State girls were competing, but we'd all swum our best at Big Tens. After training so hard all year for that big victory, no one had the energy for the same kind of performance at NCAAs, and our preliminary swims showed it. That morning we all swam well, but not our best.

That afternoon, the captain called a team meeting and we all got together in one of the hotel rooms. No coaches came, just the swimmers. While we were all sitting on the beds, the captain delivered a pep talk.

She said, "We've got to pull this together. We are all better than what we showed this morning, and we have to get it together." She talked for a few more minutes and then asked, "Does anyone have anything they'd like to add?"

I never usually spoke up at team meetings, but this time I had something to say. I raised my hand and said, "I do." All the girls turned to look at me. I took a deep breath and said, "You know, when I quit swimming, I know a lot of people might have looked down on that and thought negatively about me. But it was the one of the best decisions I ever made because I was able to take a step back from practice and meets and swimming, and really consider this sport and what it means to me. And I've come to appreciate swimming in a whole new way. Even though we swam terrible this morning, we're all still Big Ten champions. We've all accomplished great things this year, and what we do here at NCAAs isn't going to change that. Our performance today doesn't make us who we are. We're no different now than we were before we swam this morning—we're still great swimmers. So let's just go out there and enjoy ourselves."

I've never been one for pep talks, especially not since my break, and this was the first time I had talked about quitting swimming in front of the team. All the girls sat around listening to me and they were all so quiet. When I finished, they all nodded their heads and smiled at me. What I wanted them all to understand is that any sport has its ups and downs. During my swimming career, I experienced both great emotional highs and also great emotional lows. When I set the Big Ten record, broke a minute in the 100-yard breaststroke, and became Big Ten Freshman of the Year all in one night, that was an amazing high. Accomplishing all of these feats in one race sent more adrenaline through my body than anything I've ever felt. But I can also remember, when I was a sophomore at Penn State and the woman's team swam Northwestern, I placed fourth and felt so sick over my performance that I sat alone on the bus ride home and did not speak to one of my teammates. Because of my early success in swimming, I grew accustomed to first-place finishes and dropping my times in every race. I was not used to anything else and at the meet against Northwestern, I gave my all, I felt great, and the results did not make sense to me.

I worked hard to achieve what I did. My mistake was that I let my highs in swimming define me and my self-esteem. I gained self-confidence through winning, improving my times, setting records, and having a great practice. Because of my success in swimming, I had the confidence to handle schoolwork, be outgoing in social situations, and be friendly in my personal life. These traits weren't bad things to gain from a sport, but I also let my athletic lows control the way I felt about myself outside swimming. Athletes have to know how to handle the highs and keep everything in perspective. For example, in the sport of swimming, an individual can very easily have a great race and swim a personal best time, yet the team as a whole might lose the competition. In this situation, you have to be a good winner, meaning that while you enjoy your accomplishment, you have to show respect to the teammates who were not able to perform at their best. That is true sportsmanship.

The lows in sports are also a very unique and indescribable feeling. To work hard for weeks, months, and years to accomplish a specific goal and then not achieve it is devastating. Many people would say I was extremely lucky because, until college, I never really experienced a true emotional low in swimming—or in my personal life, for that matter. I was very fortunate to have a stable and wonderfully supportive family. My parents fought like anyone else's, but they had a strong marriage and supported one another and my sister and I. My entire family supported my swimming career and the choices I made at a young age to commit fully and dedicate my life to a sport. I cannot think of any one swim meet, swim practice, piano lesson, choir concert, or gymnastics meet that my parents did not attend. They were present and drove me from place to place so I could reach my potential. By the time I was a senior in high school, I was basically on my own and didn't realize I was not ready to handle any type of failure. As a result of that, I nearly lost everything I'd worked so hard to achieve.

These feelings of extreme highs and extreme lows come with being an athlete. To be an athlete, especially at a high level like a professional or collegiate athlete, these emotions can sometimes be overwhelming. When a person is young, the parents usually control the decisions for the child, like whether the child is going to attend practice every night or not. I am very thankful that my parents recognized my talent and led me down the path that allowed me to accomplish everything I did. When I was younger, I was like any kid who wanted to watch their favorite TV show instead of going to swim practice. My parents made a decision early in my career that they were going to give me the best opportunities possible to be successful and they definitely sacrificed many hours and weekends driving me all over the east coast for practice and meets. They also taught me what it meant to commit to something and stick it out.

Being an athlete also forces a child to mature quickly because of the choices they have to make and the hard work it takes to perform at your best. But I believe that to have a successful career in sports or any passion in life, you must have a healthy balance from the beginning and learn how to separate what you do from who you are. If this is achieved, then a long, happy, and successful career can definitely take place.

The challenge in any sport is to do the best you can and be happy and content with the outcome. I have always been taught not to make emotional decisions in life, and some people may have believed that quitting swimming was an emotional and rash decision. But to this day I know that it definitely was not. It was very difficult to handle the repercussions of my decision to quit, for example, the anger and sadness that my parents felt and the disappointment of my teammates and coaches. I never would have appreciated swimming if I hadn't stopped when I did. I could have gone on being a regular student and enjoyed my last couple years in college, focusing on my education and discovering new interests and talents. But instead I was forced to see swimming from an outside perceptive and rediscover the love and passion I had when I first started.

When I swam the weekend of NCAAs, I knew that was my last meet. On Monday I would be retired from swimming, and although that would be another big life change, I was mentally ready to be done. I swam as hard as I could, but the way we'd trained and tapered for Big Tens, I knew I wasn't going to do anything extraordinary that weekend. But I had fun and tried my best to enjoy every minute—something I didn't know how to do three years before. Back then, I was faced with a crossroad, I made a decision despite how everyone around me felt, and I learned numerous lessons from the challenges that arose from it. Being able to stand up for something that you feel is right and that you know in your heart is what will make you happy is something very special.

After my last race, the 200 breast the last morning of the meet, I met my parents in the lobby outside the pool area. My dad was smiling and trying to choke back tears. He wrapped his arms around me and gave me a long hug, and then he looked at me and said, "Thank you, Kris, for the last seventeen years. It was a fun ride."

The challenges in life are what help us grow and discover our true character. Page: 119

Many people looked negatively on my decision to quit, but it made me who I am today. It changed how I looked at life and I won't ever forget about it because I never want to go back to that place. Instead of looking back on it and feeling embarrassed, I'm proud of it because it helped make me a stronger character.

As kids go through hardships and need time away, it's not a weakness and they shouldn't feel guilty about it. When you force yourself to go go go, that's when burnout happens. You have to have a balance in life. If you can catch the signs early enough, you can lessen the effects on the person and their ability to participate in their sport. In addition to the stress of competition, practice, and outside expectations, young athletes experience stress when they transition into college and when they face life after sport. Just the thought of having your career over after college is a hard thing to come to grips with. I know I struggled with how to deal with not to be a swimmer anymore. One of the main reasons I fought with Bill and didn't get best times was because I wasn't living in the moment. I kept wondering, does all this hard work and dedication really matter when college will be over and my career will be done. Would I have anything else after swimming was over? I never thought about getting good grades, or getting an internship, and I lived day to day in the sport. When that's all you've ever thought about, you struggle to be in society.

Quitting was the first decision I made on my own—going to Penn State, going to China, and many of the other decisions about my career were made by other people. I didn't believe I had anything once swimming was done, and I wanted to show people that I could do it. When I started struggling with these issues, no one took me seriously. So when I quit it was kind of a way to show that I really wasn't joking—I was having a hard time and I stood up for myself. No one believed I'd do it. Not my coaches, not my teammates, and especially not my parents. But I had to—the rest of my career depended on it.

As the three of us left the pool that day and headed for lunch together, I knew then that regardless of what had happened in the past, I was ready for the future, I was ready for retirement, and I was ready for whatever challenge I would face next.

How to Identify the Symptoms of Mental Health Issues in Athletes
Tips for Parents, Coaches, and Teammates

My primary reason for writing this book was to help parents and coaches identify athletes who are at risk or are experiencing symptoms of mental health issues. Like most medical problems, early identification of mental illness usually means less disruption to an athlete's life, fewer severe health complications, and a less complicated, quicker recovery. I've compiled the following list of tips based on my own experiences and research from mental health professionals, particularly a report, "Managing Student-Athlete's Mental Health Issues," put together by Ron A. Thompson, Ph.D., and Roberta Trattner Sherman, Ph.D., FAED, from the Bloomington Center for Counseling and Human Development Bloomington, Indiana.

According to their research, an athlete's mental health is often considered secondary to physical health. When athletes are physically injured, there's a network of supporters to help them recover. But if an athlete experiences depression, burnout, or another mental health issues, they are often left to struggle on their own.

Knowing how to identify and respond to mental health issues can help prevent larger problems from developing, and it can help your athletes perform their best. Here's a few suggestions on what to do.

1. **Know the symptoms of mental health issues, which include:**

Behavior Symptoms
Social withdrawal
Irresponsibility
Legal issues
Difficulty with authority
Decrement in sport or academic performance

Cognitive Symptoms
Confusion/difficulty making decisions
All-or-nothing thinking
Negative self-talk

Emotional/Psychological Symptoms
Mood swings
Excessive worry or fear
Agitation/irritability
Low self-esteem
Lack of motivation

Physical/Medical Symptoms
Sleep difficulty
Shaking and trembling
Fatigue, tiredness, weakness

2. Respond with understanding, support, and reassurance. After looking back on my swimming career, I realized that because of my unbalanced life and overtraining syndrome (brought on by heavy training without breaks or rest), I struggled with depression and anxiety. If parents, coaches, or athletes see these signs and symptoms, considerable support and reassurance is needed. Most often than not, the athlete experiencing mental health issues is tired and even exhausted by their symptoms. And the athlete is probably looking for some kind of relief.

3. Understand that mental health issues are not weaknesses. The most serious mistake that anyone can make in dealing with an athlete with mental health issues is to respond to the problems as trivial or a sign of weakness. Unfortunately, this is often the way mental health issues are handled in athletics. The coach, parent, or friend must accept that it is a serious problem and listen to the athlete.

4. When an athlete approaches you about emotional or mental issues, listen. If someone comes to you with a problem, it's an indication that they are struggling and need to talk. They are reaching out and looking for help, so don't dismiss it.

5. Refer the athlete to a mental health professional who can help. A sports psychologist, psychiatrist, or counselor will know how best to handle the problem.

6. Communicate! Simply asking how the athlete is feeling, how school is going, and how practice is going is a great way to show the athlete that you care and are willing to listen and help them recover. This approach with hopefully also help the athlete open up and talk about the difficulties they are having, which is the first step to finding a solution to the mental health problems.

Balancing the high demands of a sport with other aspects of life can be more challenging than any competition. The mind and body are connected, so if an athlete's mental health isn't as strong as it should be, there's no way he or she can compete at an optimum level. If an athlete is struggling with an emotional or mental health issue, he or she may feel like no one in the world can help. Just knowing the symptoms and being there for support can make a huge difference in an athlete's situation, and their performance!